POLYGAMY UNDER ATTACK

From Tom Green to Brian David Mitchell

by John R. Llewellyn

Polygamy Under Attack: From Tom Green to Brian David Mitchell
by John R. Llewellyn

Publisher's Cataloging-in-Publication Data

Llewellyn, John R.
    Polygamy under attack : from Tom Green to Brian David Mitchell / John R. Llewellyn. – 1st ed.
        p.cm
        LCCN: 2003117091
        ISBN: 1-888106-76-X

1. Polygamy–Religious aspects–Mormon Church–history. 2. Marriage–Religious aspects–Church of Jesus Christ of Latter-day Saints. I. Title
        BX8641.S26   2004289.3'092

Printed in the United States of America

Agreka™ Books LLC
(800) 360-5284
www.agreka.com

Dedication

To my Children, Grandchildren, and
Great Grandchildren to come.

Acknowledgements

I wish to acknowledge the generous and valuable contributions of all those who have made this book possible. During the Tom Green trial, Utah Attorney General Investigators Ron Barton and Diana Hollis provided valuable information. Scrutinizing the seamy side of the FLDS would have been impossible without the expert assistance of Ron Barton and historian Ben Bistline. I owe much to Vicky Prunty and Rowenna Erickson of Tapestry Against Polygamy. Bob Curran and his crew at Help The Child Brides have been helpful in many ways.

A special thanks to Attorney General Mark Shurtleff who put politics aside and dared to do what no other elected official has attempted since 1953. I want to thank my son-in-law Rob Thompson and his brother James for their valuable contributions. And my co-investigator and good buddy, Rod Williams. For over four years we rooted out convincing evidence that helped Virginia Hill win her lawsuit. And a special thanks to a special friend, David Bishop, a good cop and an excellent student of Mormon history. Whenever I got stumped I could always turn to him.

Others I wish to thank: David Leavitt, Monte Stewart, Bill Aldrich, Rena Mackert, Laura Chapman, and a friend and confident in the Kingston Clan. Some in the Allred Group, whose names it would not be wise to mention. There are countless others I could list and I am grateful for all their ideas, opinions, and suggestions.

A writer can get grumpy when he has trouble finding the right word or right phrase. So I need to thank my lovely wife Shauna, for putting up with me.

Contents

After sitting through the trial and providing testimony for Juab County prosecutor David Leavitt as he convicted Tom Green of child rape, I began working on this book. As I continued writing, other Polygamy Fundamentalists kept leaping into the headlines with stories of abuse.

Then came the worldwide bombshell of Brian David Mitchell, the itinerant sidewalk preacher who kidnaped Elizabeth Smart. The entire world had been focused on publicity hungry Tom Green and his claim of a *peaceful life* as a polygamist, when Mitchell and his accomplice wife shocked the world by their crime against Elizabeth Smart.

These highly publicized cases brought the world's attention to modern-day abuses that many thought only existed in third world countries. The abuses gained so much attention that Oprah Winfrey aired a segment on abusive polygamy in Utah and Arizona, and followed with an interview of Elizabeth and her family in the Smart's home.

Mounting public concern caused me to realize that people were finally ready to become informed about the practices of each of the Mormon Fundamentalist groups, what they do, and *why they say they do it.* Organized anti-polygamy groups need public support as they press the government to find realistic solutions.

As a result of all the publicity, Arizona and Utah are taking a hard look at the human rights violations, not to mention the millions of dollars of state and federal welfare money that support the groups when polygamist wives – claiming to be single mothers with children – sign up for welfare benefits. One informant reported that her welfare checks are often taken directly to the priesthood leaders of their group.

Concerned citizens need to understand that all these polygamists – Tom Green, Brian David Mitchell, David Kingston, and others – have a motivating common denominator from the 1800s. While the mainstream LDS Church abandoned polygamy a century ago, there are thousands of dissidents practicing plural marriage, who call themselves Mormon Fundamentalists.

This book will examine how what is a sacred belief to many people has been criminalized by some of the men within the Fundamentalist Groups. The question every decent citizen must ask: What can be done about it? What will, or can, Utah and the neighboring state of Arizona actually do, if anything? What resources are available. The victims are not just young girls, but women and men too, conditioned from birth to endure abuse under the guise of religious beliefs. They don't know what to do or where to go.

It is my hope that this book will enlighten society so that the abuses within these groups can be targeted for action, in particular the young girls forced into a plural marriage with men old enough to be their father. In one group, incest is encouraged to "keep a pure blood line."

To make these girls and women become real to unenlightened citizens, I wrote an emotionally-charged and tender fact-based novel *A Teenager's Tears: When Parents Convert to Polygamy*. I wanted people to be able to walk in their shoes and feel what they feel, to be on the inside looking out.

It is important to understand that the vast majority of polygamists do not represent a criminal threat to the peace and dignity of American principles. They feel that plural marriage should be decriminalized. And many involved in dealing with the abuses believe that decriminalizing plural marriage would remove the veil of secrecy that allows these abuses to go on, so read the chapter on Decriminalizing Polygamy. With recent Supreme Court decisions, many believe that plural marriage has a good chance to gain legal acceptance.

Those involved in plural marriage who conduct their lives with dignity and respect are as outraged at the abuses as everyone else. This book is intended to help the public and law enforcement better understand what goes on and how it develops. Before solutions can be found, one must first understand the intricate problems involved.

America was founded on religious freedom and individual rights. The government must find a way to preserve these for each citizen, without trampling on the rights we hold so dear.

Chapter One

A Brief History of the Mormon Fundamentalist World

In Utah, Arizona, and neighboring states, even into Canada and Mexico, polygamy practice stems from early Mormon beliefs. Even though not condoned since the late 1800s by The Church of Jesus Christ of Latter-day Saints (LDS), thousands of people still practice polygamy today and claim it is the true "Mormonism."

For over a century The Church of Jesus Christ of Latter-day Saints has been known as the Mormon Church, because of their scripture book, the Book of Mormon. But according to current President Gordon B. Hinckley, prophet and leader of the LDS Church, *Mormon* is a pseudonym that is no longer spiritually acceptable or politically correct. He has asked the media to discontinue referring to the LDS Church as the Mormon Church.

President Hinckley has repeatedly declared that these polygamists are not, and should not be, linked to the LDS Church. When members of the Church are discovered practicing polygamy, they are promptly excommunicated.

But two important facts that complicate the issue should be understood – the LDS Church still believes in the divinity of plural marriage in heaven, even while it no longer allows members to practice it on earth. And a significant percentage of faithful members of the LDS Church have ancestors who practiced polygamy. Thus, members of the LDS Church today are conflicted over the way some modern-day polygamists should be dealt with.

In Utah and Arizona, members of the LDS Church can be

found in government positions, law enforcement, etc., and of course they have mixed feelings about the issue of polygamists. Most people recognize that there are polygamist families who truly believe they are living as God wants them to, thus "religious freedom" comes into play.

What we wish to do in this book is teach and inform our citizenry of the hidden abuses that occur, that such abuses are not found in every family, but where they are found, they must be dealt with. We can no longer turn our heads and pretend it will all go away. It isn't going away.

Because the polygamists call themselves Mormon Fundamentalists, the word "Mormonisn" is found, heard, and spoken throughout the Fundamentalist world and is necessarily included in this book. There is simply no other word to describe the belief system that underlies plural marriage as found in our part of the world.

The intricate tapestry that makes up the Mormon Fundamentalist subculture can be confusing to a person unfamiliar with Mormonism. There are a number of established groups. Each "group" has its own mode of thought, and each believes it is the jewel of Mormonism, much like Sunnism and Shi'ism, the 'Abbasids and Ba'th Party are to Islam. Therefore, I will attempt to untangle any confusion and give the reader an idea how each group or individual fits into the whole picture.

Let's examine the history of the Mormon Fundamentalist movement. The Fundamentalists rejected the LDS Church's contention that a contemporary revelation or prophet can negate or suspend the revelation of an earlier prophet, in this case, Joseph Smith.

In 1890 Prophet Wilford Woodruff issued a Manifesto prohibiting the further practice of plural marriage which, according to the Church, suspended that portion of the 132nd Section of the D&C that mandated the practice of polygamy. (The LDS Church scriptures are comprised of three standard works: the Book of

Mormon, the Doctrine and Covenants [D&C], and the Pearl of Great Price.) The Fundamentalist position is, if God has not abrogated the practice, and according to the early leaders of the Church, God said he would never abrogate polygamy, then it ought to be lived.

The 1890 Woodruff manifesto ceasing the practice of polygamy is entitled "Official Declaration." The Declaration can be found in the D & C following the 136th Section. Some members of the Church at that time thought the Manifesto was a trick, a pretense that would fool the United States Government and convince them that the LDS Church was committed to ending polygamy, so Utah statehood could follow. But, in fact, it was real.

Mormon Fundamentalism Develops

It wasn't until after the turn of the century that all members of the Church fully complied with the Manifesto.[1] Then in the 1920s a group of disgruntled Mormons began to hold secret meetings debating the consequences of the LDS Church abandoning "celestial marriage." A fellow named Lorin Woolley showed up at one of the meetings with a fantastic tale, a tale which pro and con historians still endlessly explore.

He claimed that in 1886 while guarding the prophet who was in hiding from federal marshals, LDS Prophet John Taylor received a supernatural visitation from Joseph Smith and Jesus Christ. Joseph and the Lord placed President Taylor under covenant to keep alive plural marriage until the Second Coming. The following day, President Taylor held a meeting, which has gone down in Fundamentalist history as "The Eight Hour Meeting."

From that momentous meeting, thousands of former Mormons have justified the continuous practice of polygamy in spite of the LDS Church mandate and laws of the land.

By 1929 the Lorin Woolly story had been refined and edited into plausible fact so that practicing polygamists could honestly say, "I am just living my religion, I'm just carrying out the will of God, it is the only way I can hope to go to the celestial kingdom."(Mormons believe in three heavens, the telestial, terrestrial, and celestial, with celestial being the highest. Within the celestial heaven are three degrees.) Fundamentalists believe that only those who live polygamy will get to the highest degree. They refer to D&C Sections 76 and 131.)

These believers in the alleged 1886 Revelation were still a clandestine group in 1929. And as with any group, a leader must surface. Lorin Woolly became that man.[2] But in "Mormonism" a leader must also have priesthood authority (a bestowal from God), so plausible authority was invented. Non-fundamentalist historians have given the credit of manufacturing priesthood authority to Joseph Musser, who became the leader of all Mormon Fundamentalists in the 1930s.

The following scenario spiritually contrived by Musser is paraphrased:

> The priesthood and church are two separate entities, each have their explicit calling. The Eight Hour Meeting gave the fundamentalists the priesthood and the priesthood is to the church what the husband is to the wife. The church calling is missionary work, spreading the gospel throughout the world; the priesthood calling is to keep alive the practice of plural marriage.

For years the more honorable modern day polygamist leaders like Rulon C. Allred were very supportive of the mainstream LDS Church. But in 1978 that all changed when the LDS Church issued another Official Declaration permitting male members of the Black Race to hold the priesthood.

Fundamentalists were outraged. They perceived the declaration as another example of the LDS Church caving in to political pressure. It was the last straw. First the Church disbanded the "Council of Fifty," the government of God. Then they discontinued the United Order, a form of communalism. Next came plural marriage, the most sacred of all of God's principles; and finally by giving the priesthood to the Black Race.[3]

The various fundamentalist leaders (each called himself a prophet) over the several polygamist groups were for once in agreement. They predicted that the temples would be polluted and Black men would be taking white women as wives. They believed it was the final and greatest insult to the memory of Joseph Smith and Brigham Young.

But behind that mask of rage, the fundamentalist prophets were delighted. It was the catalyst they had been waiting for, the excuse to supplant the Church, and wrestle away what was left of the LDS Church's priesthood authority.

The fundamentalist ranks swelled as many disenchanted, conservative Mormons defected over the Black issue. The organized groups, especially Apostolic United Brethren, built their own temples and went into competition with the LDS Church for members and tithing. However, each organized polygamist group leader claimed that the "keys" belonged to him, and according to the D & C, only one man on earth at a time can hold the keys.

Priesthood authority within the Mormon concept is a nebulous concept that has power only when the laity recognizes the authority. It's not like a stick of dynamite that the prophet carries around coercing the laity to conform or else. The authority is intangible and invisible, but it can be just as deadly as a stick of dynamite under the control of a fundamentalist fanatic like mass murderer Ervil LeBaron.[4] Priesthood authority is a concept without force unless accepted by its followers. Authority is defined in Verse 7 of the 132nd Section of the D & C, and states that only one person on earth at a time can hold the "keys" of the priesthood.

Verse 7 is the single most important passage in the Doctrine & Covenants because in that passage is vested all power. However, there is a problem: the "keys" of authority are indistinct to the senses. The only way they can be detected is by the "spirit" (a supernatural manifestation), or by physical and psychological submission to authority.

In order to understand the motives of Mormon Fundamentalists, one must have an understanding of the *keys of priesthood authority.* Only "one" man, the prophet, seer and revelator, the one holding the keys, has the authority to collect tithing, seal plural marriages for time and all eternity, and give the endowment (a temple ritual). Money, marriage, and temple are the foundation or power of Mormon Fundamentalism. It is in the temple that the endowment is given and the place where celestial marriages are sealed.[5] The priesthood keys gives *one man* power over the very exaltation of those who submit to his authority. According to Verse 7, the prophet has power over every aspect of the true believer's life, that is of course, if the prophet can convince the true believer he alone holds the coveted keys.

At the present time there are dozens of men who portend to be the *one* holding the keys. Gordon B. Hinckley, president of the LDS Church, tops the list because he is the most powerful, but that doesn't discourage ambitious fundamentalist usurpers from scrambling to attract a following and collect their share of the glory and tithing.

It is estimated that there are between 25 and 100 thousand polygamists in and around Utah. In the author's opinion there are no more than 30 thousand and that's pushing it. Some pundits deliberately inflate the numbers to make it appear the polygamists are more powerful, or the problem is worse than it really is.

In the early days Joseph Musser, living in Salt Lake City, was the recognized fundamentalist leader of all the people practicing polygamy, no matter where they actually lived. They referred to themselves as "living the principle."

In about 1926 Leroy Johnson (also called Roy and Uncle Roy) helped pioneer a settlement in a remote, inhospitable Arizona desert called Short Creek. The town was renamed Colorado City[6] in 1961. Their population expanded west across the Utah border and formed Hildale, Utah. It looks like one community from the air.

In the early days there came a time when disagreements developed among the people and a split occurred. The debate as to who was right continues to this day. Nevertheless, nearly all of the organized polygamist groups evolved either directly or indirectly from that split. A detailed explanation of all that unfolded from the very beginning is contained in *The Polygamists: A History of Colorado City, Arizona* by historian Ben Bistline, who lived through it all. Today there are a number of groups and you will read details about each of them throughout this book.

The central theme of all the organized Mormon Fundamentalist groups is plural marriage, or more correctly, polygyny, and is the axis around which the fundamentalist world revolves. It is powerful dogma. If you believe that Joseph Smith was a prophet, then you must believe that plural marriage is God's word to the Mormons. It is said that Joseph Smith was an illiterate farm boy who couldn't have invented the Book of Mormon, but in reading the writings of Joseph, unless it has been carefully edited, it is not the writings of an uneducated, inarticulate boy. Mormonism is sophisticated doctrine.

Chapter Two

A Profile of Each Group and the Independents

Corporation of the President of the Fundamentalist Church of Jesus Christ of Latter-day Saints (FLDS)

Utah Department of Commerce transcript #149512, organized 2-6-91

Population: About 10 thousand

Priesthood leader: currently, Warren Jeffs

The Corp. of the President of the Fundamentalist Church is colloquially known as FLDS and is the largest of Utah's polygamist groups. Members of the FLDS used to be scattered throughout Utah and Arizona until 2001, when Warren Jeffs instructed the faithful to sell out and move to Colorado City, Arizona.

The FLDS routinely sends their young men on two-year work missions. These boys are placed on jobs usually controlled by the priesthood leaders of the group and their paychecks go to the priesthood. In exchange the boys are promised a wife and a building lot on priesthood-owned ground.

According to Rulon Jeffs (who it is said married nineteen women and fathered sixty children), when young girls reach marriageable age they are expected to present themselves to the priesthood for placement as a wife in a family. All marriages are controlled by the priesthood, neither the boy nor the girl has a choice. When a girl in the FLDS is biologically mature enough to bear children, she is married off. Reluctant girls have been known to disappear and resurface years later with one or two children.

Some girls, like Flora Jessop, have been held prisoner in their bedrooms for weeks or months on end until they consent.[7]

Colorado City, Arizona, is located on Highway 389 near the Utah border. Hildale, Utah, on Highway 59 is the sister-city of Colorado City. Both towns are incorporated and owned lock, stock, and barrel by the United Effort Plan, a *land trust* controlled by a priesthood hierarchy.

The United Effort Plan (UEP) was created with good intentions but opponents say it has developed into a devilish legal instrument with which to coerce and control members who have built on UEP property. Members of the FLDS are invited to build homes on UEP property, *at their own expense.* After the dwellings are completed, the UEP believed they had the power to evict a member from his home without just cause and without reimbursing him. A prolonged court battle resulted over the UEP's ownership of the land and its unfair use of power. (This type of legal instrument and the power it gives leaders of a group is discussed more fully under Communities of Apostolic United Brethren, CAUB, the land trust operated by the AUB.)

In 1984 a split occurred in the priesthood hierarchy over the United Effort Plan, and LeRoy Johnson's one man, tyrannical rule.

The split resulted in a long, protracted lawsuit filed in 1987 when LeRoy Johnson and Rulon Jeffs tried to evict families from their property, who would not recognize their priesthood authority. The two factions became known as Ward 1 and Ward 2. Ward 2 was the smaller faction.

The dissidents in Ward 2 moved south across Arizona Highway 389 and began developing a new settlement named Centennial Park. Ward 2 organized their own priesthood hierarchy under the leadership of Johnny Timpson, and is now considered a group separate from the FLDS. They are referred to as Ward 2 or the Centennial Park group.

In Ward 1, LeRoy died in 1986 leaving Rulon Jeffs in charge. Rulon died in 2002 leaving his son Warren in charge. For various reasons, not everyone in Colorado City or Centennial Park is a practicing polygamist, although they do believe in the religious principle.

Colorado City, Arizona, and Hildale, Utah, are legally incorporated entities entitled to all the prestige, privileges, and government grants as other cities of equal size. They have taken advantage of government grants in improving their roads, developing their water supply, and expanding their airport.

Although the roads are public domain, the land on which all the houses and commercial buildings are erected are owned by the UEP. The mayor form of government that manages these two cities is nothing more than a veneer for the actual government, which is the UEP. The trustees of the UEP are comprised of the FLDS theocracy. (A Priesthood is typically comprised of the leader or prophet, his two counselors, and ten council members.)

According to FLDS apostates, the mayor and police department function at the will of the council. The police officers use their authority to enforce the edicts of the priesthood council. They protect the constitutional rights of the citizenry only when those rights do not conflict with the will of the priesthood. According to dissidents, the police harass and bully undesirables with the intent of driving them out of the communities.

Neither the FLDS nor Centennial Park Fundamentalists give the endowment, the special ritual performed in the temple. The FLDS takes the position that the practice of polygamy is sufficient to allow entrance into the highest degree of the celestial kingdom.

The combined population of the FLDS and Centennial Park is estimated to be about 10,000.

Corporation of the Presiding Elder of Apostolic United Brethren (AUB)

Utah Department of Commerce transcript # 149512, organized 3-14-75.

Population: Between 5000 and 7000

Registered Agent: Owen A. Allred

Location: Bluffdale, Utah, at the Jordan Narrows near Camp Williams.

The Corp. of the Presiding Elder of Apostolic United Brethren, colloquially known as Apostolic United Brethren, or AUB, is the second largest, organized polygamist group in Utah with between 5000 and 7000 members. The membership fluctuates as converts come and go like a revolving door.

In August 1997, Virginia Hill filed a lawsuit in the Second Judicial District Court, Juab County, Nephi, Utah, against AUB, Owen A. Allred and others, accusing them of stealing 1.54 million dollars in cash.

It is of interest that both the FLDS and AUB have copied the LDS Church format for their corporations: Corporation of the President of The Church of Jesus Christ of Latter-day Saints. The fundamentalist are great copiers. Owen Allred, in his attempt to supplant the LDS Church, has structured his organization identical to the LDS Church. After the LDS Church opened the priesthood doors to the Black race, AUB converted a duplex into a temple and now give their own version of the Temple Endowment. They are also performing baptisms for the dead.

In observing new converts to AUB, I believe that most men who enter the group have their own secret agenda: power, women, adventure, intellectualism, unification, leadership, etc. Mormon Fundamentalism provides access to all those passions or desires. Once entrenched in the AUB society, it is quite common for these men to bear testimony that they unequivocally believe that the principle of plural marriage is a divine commandment and that the prophet (Owen Allred) holds the keys to the kingdom of heaven. If these men are unable to satisfy their secret agendas, they leave.

This is one reason AUB has such a large turnover of converts.

I am convinced that ambitious converts use testimony to ingratiate themselves with both leadership and the membership. The more pious and submissive the convert appears, the more he is trusted by leadership and women. Women in AUB are attracted by power, piety, quixotism, and affluence.

AUB has the following enclaves

Pinesdale, Montana, is an incorporated city located just north and west of Hamilton in the beautiful Bitter Root Valley. Pinesdale boasts about 1000 inhabitants. Marvin Jessop and his brother Morris are the priesthood leaders who preside over the town's elected officials. Pinesdale, like Colorado City and Hildale, has received government grants towards the improvement of the town. And according to reliable informants inside Pinesdale, like Colorado City, plural wives are sent into nearby Hamilton to apply for welfare as single mothers. The informant reported that welfare checks are often taken directly to the priesthood leaders.

Rocky Ridge, Utah, is an incorporated town in Juab County located just south of the town of Santaquin on I-15. Rocky Ridge is an easily recognized cluster of large, multifamily dwellings on the side of the hill just west of the Freeway. About 300 habitants, counting women and children, live at Rocky Ridge.

The Granite Ranch, a dairy farm, is another enclave of AUB, located in the west desert of Snake Valley in Juab County near the Nevada border. According to AUB's accountant, about thirty cents of every tithing dollar is funneled out to the Granite Ranch, amounting to approximately $300,000 a year. About ten families live and work on the Granite. Glen Allred, Owen's favorite son, manages the ranch.

Pleasant Valley, Nevada, is a cluster of ramshackle, mice-infested trailers on a sagebrush hill about fifteen miles southwest of the Granite Ranch just inside the Nevada border. In 1997 there were eight families living at Pleasant Valley.

Motoqua, Utah, is a ragtag rural community of about ten families sequestered in a large ravine south of St. George, Utah. Motoqua is located about five miles as the crow flies from the Desert Inn Ranch, which also played a vital role in the Hill vs. Allred lawsuit.

Ozumba, Mexico, is the Mexican branch of AUB with a population of about 700. Ozumba has its own temple and is visited by the AUB council twice a year. Mexican nationalists, adherents to AUB, are smuggled back and forth across the border on a regular bases.

There are about thirty polygamist families who live approximately ten miles west of Cedar City, Utah.

AUB Subordinate Corporations

1. Red Cedar Corporation, Utah Dept. of Commerce #126836. Date of Incorporation: 7-15-87. Registered agent: Glen Allred.

Red Cedar Corporation is the legal owner of the Granite Ranch. Owen Allred, Glen Allred, and J. LaMoine Jenson are the officers of Red Cedar. Until 1994 when fellow investigator Rod Williams and I discovered the existence of Red Cedar, the AUB membership was led to believe that the Granite was owned directly by AUB. Members had been asked to pay double tithes to help make payments on the Granite and to donate free labor. Young men on work missions were often sent to labor on the ranch. These loyal members were told they were helping to build the kingdom of God, but in reality it was a kingdom for Owen and Glen Allred. And when the membership found out they had been deceived, it didn't seem to faze them a bit. They went on paying their tithing and AUB went on sending hundreds of thousands of dollars out to the ranch to keep it operational – because Owen A. Allred held the keys to the kingdom.

2. Unified Industries, Utah Dept. Commerce # 08211

The officers of Unified Industries (UI) are the same officers as AUB.

Unified Industries was originally filed May 24, 1979, as a non profit "church auxiliary to provide charitable welfare relief in connection with religious worship and Christian fellowship." However, in 1985, UI lost its tax exempt status. In depth investigation shows that the only time UI was ever charitable is when it bailed out the AUB hierarchy from failed business ventures. The AUB hierarchy has a long list of failed enterprises. However, what they lack in business skills they make up in selling Mormon Fundamentalism to new converts and collecting their ten percent tithes.

The current leader of AUB is Owen A. Allred, who inherited the position when his older brother Rulon C. Allred was murdered by rival polygamist Ervil LeBaron. Due to the advanced years and poor health of Owen Allred, council member J. LaMoine Jenson, owner and manager of Jenson Lumber in Draper, Utah, has been named by Allred to succeed him. It is reported that the selection of Jenson as priesthood leader does not sit well with Marvin Jessop, the AUB priesthood leader over Pinesdale, Montana. Jessop believes he is senior to Jenson, consequently AUB insiders are predicting that Montana will split from AUB when Allred dies.

Unified Industries in essence is the banking institution of AUB. Although its funding comes from AUB tithing monies, it does negotiate loans among privileged members and collects interest. For many years all the property owned by AUB was placed under the care and custody of Unified Industries. For example, the town of Pinesdale, Montana, was once owned by AUB, then transferred into UI. During that time it was proper and permissible for a tenant living at Pinesdale to sell his improvement (home) to another member. But that all came to an end in 1994.

3. Communities of Apostolic United Brethren, #170153

Incorporated July 6, 1994, Registered agent: M. Kent Allred

The Communities of Apostolic United Brethren, better known as CAUB, is Owen Allred's answer to the FLDS United Effort Plan (UEP). All of the AUB property that was recorded in the name of Unified Industries is now recorded under Communities of Apostolic United Brethren (CAUB).

At this juncture, I will explain the importance of the legal entities UEP and CAUB.

The UEP: A lawsuit developed among the people of Colorado City and Hildale against the United Effort Plan land trust ruled over by Rulon Jeffs. They claimed that the followers of FLDS were encouraged to build homes on UEP property and were told that their homes would be safe from outside forces, that no one would ever be able to take their homes away from them. However, there was a hidden snare. The legal instrument labeled occupants as "tenants at will." As tenants at will, Rulon Jeffs had the power to evict a family without compensating them for "improvements," meaning the cost of materials and labor in building the house. Utilizing that power, Jeffs began evicting those families who were considered undesirables or disloyal to him or his priesthood. They were left with nothing.

The FLDS became divided over Jeff's capricious use of power. Those opposed to the UEP filed a lawsuit, separated themselves from the main group, and became known as Ward 2. They moved their headquarters across the highway in what is now called Centennial Park.

After millions of dollars in legal fees, the controversy was finally decided by the Utah Supreme Court in September 1998. Justice Zimmerman issued the following opinion:

> In essence, the UEP could not evict an occupant without reimbursing him for his improvements. The occupant could not deed or bequeath his interest to a third party. When the occupant died, the improvement became the property of the UEP. If the occupant abandoned the improvement it became the property of the UEP.

The CAUB: Its bylaws now plug up the loophole of having to reimburse evicted occupants for their "improvements."

In 1997 members living on CAUB property were required to sign an "occupancy agreement." CAUB owns the town of

Pinesdale, Montana, and a subdivision named Harvest Haven in Utah County. The CAUB bishop of each community made the rounds informing the occupants they must sign the agreement. Many signed without reading the agreement, trusting in their bishop to always act in their best interest. But a few refused to sign.

Towards the bottom of the "occupancy agreement" is a clause that states (paraphrased)

> In the event the occupant is found to be out of harmony with the bishop, the occupant can be evicted with or without reimbursement.

In essence, those who signed the occupancy agreement have placed their homes under the capricious control of CAUB. The few who refused to sign were held in contempt and ostracized. Those who signed can no longer sell their "improvements." Thus if a member of the AUB decides to leave, he must walk away without any financial reimbursement for his house. The occupancy agreement has not been tested in the courts.

4. Big Valley Credit Union

Big Valley Credit Union is an exclusive AUB credit union located at 147 West 12300 South, Draper, Utah, which also happens to be the location of Jenson Lumber. In 1994 the registered agent of Big Valley Credit Union was LaMoine Jenson's plural wife Violet. LaMoine is the priesthood councilman assigned to oversee the credit union and is a loan officer. During the 1970s when the author was on the board of Big Valley, Jenson Lumber was dependent upon loans from the credit union. The principal member of Big Valley, with the largest deposits amounting to thousands of dollars, was AUB. When LaMoine Jenson needed Big Valley money to keep his lumber business operational, a moratorium was placed on all other loans. In essence, Big Valley was LaMoine Jenson's private loaning institution. Other members were granted loans only when Jenson didn't need the money.

In summary, AUB pursues the following objectives.

First, to keep alive the fundamental beliefs and practices introduced by Joseph Smith, primarily plural marriage. Second, to convince members that all priesthood authority has been taken away from the LDS Church and given to AUB. Third, that AUB is the only religious institution with the authority to seal celestial marriages, in other words, marriage for time and all eternity, which includes monogamous as well as plural marriages. Fourth, that AUB has the true endowment and is the only entity authorized by God to perform baptisms for the dead. They teach that baptisms for the dead performed by the LDS Church are no longer efficacious. Fifth, all tithing should go to AUB for the support of AUB and the building of the kingdom of God.

AUB is typical of all the organized polygamist groups. The doctrines, land trusts, corporations, temple blessings, and incorporated towns are all structured to augment and advance the power base of the group leader and his hierarchy.

Latterday Church of Christ (The Kingston Co–op Group)

The Latterday Church of Christ, transcript #175422, incorporated 12-27-77

Population: Approximately 1000

Registered Agent: Merlin B. Kingston.

The Latterday Church is the third largest, most obscure, and fanatically frugal of the Mormon Fundamentalist groups. It is best known as the Kingston Clan, because the hierarchy consists exclusively of Kingston progeny. At this writing, Merlin Kingston is the only surviving brother of Charles Eldon Kingston, the original Kingston who separated from Joseph Musser in 1935 and started up the economic, quasi-united order that is the Kingston organization.

When Ortel Kingston died in 1987, Merlin was pushed aside as leader by Ortel's son Paul Kingston. Paul is reported to have at least thirty-two wives and more than 200 children. Besides his duties as spiritual leader and CEO of the Kingston conglomerate, he finds time to deliver all his own infant children as well as many others in the group. According to Paul there are about 1000 members in the Kingston group.

The Kingstons are the most private and probably the wealthiest of the organized polygamist groups. Unlike the FLDS that is isolated geographically, the Kingstons blend with mainstream society in Salt Lake and Davis Counties. It is their compulsion for privacy (interrupted as secrecy) that isolates them.

The Clan is best known for their *extreme* frugality and dozens and dozens of corporations in Utah, Arizona, Colorado, New Mexico, and Nevada.

Kingston frugality deserves a description. Thrift among the Kingstons is considered a virtue. What appears to be indigence to an outsider is actually godliness. The clapboard house, paint peeling, cardboard over broken windows, junk cars and debris instead of grass and flowers is not an uncommon domicile for the plural wife of a high-ranking Kingstonite. What you see as impecuniousness is really the antithesis of conspicuous consumption, frugality in the extreme. What looks like a hovel and wretched surroundings is really a monastery of righteousness.

The many dark-haired, humbly dressed children bearing remarkably noble Kingston genetic characteristics may not know the name of their father. If the child doesn't know who his father is, he can't testify and a polygamist relationship cannot be proved. The mother makes due with bare necessities, while the father and husband is a glorified example of thrift, a paragon of the group.

According to Rowenna Erickson, the first leader of the group, Eldon Kingston, initiated what was called "sacrificial humility" (a voluntary asceticism) withdrawing below all things and then working one's way back up. What began as judicious ascetics turned into an instrument of control and the members were kept at the bottom.

But like many institutions there is a double standard. The late Ortell Kingston (the leader who followed Eldon) while presiding over his Clan was the epitome of humility and set the yardstick of frugality for the group, a paradigm that no one was expected to exceed. For years, he wore the same sport coat to church, and made a pair of shoes last twenty years. When he went to China on business, he returned impressed with the quality of Chinese poverty, a judicious model lower than his. But it is said that when he did business with mainstream society he wore fine suits, shirts, and ties fitting his executive position. If dressing like a Wall Street executive enhanced his ability to make money, then he was not above lowering his high standard of abject frugality.

Their many businesses include restaurant supply, garbage disposal, pawn shops, family retail stores, and ranching. Merlin Kingston managed the Wine Cup and Gamble Ranches north and east of Wells, Nevada. The two ranches, running east to west, stretched fifty miles. For some reason, probably lack of profit, in 2003 they let the leases expire.

Among the most notable business is a large coal mine near Huntington, Utah. According to Merlin Kingston, they exported coal as far away as China. In October 2003 approximately seventy Latino miners demonstrated against the Co-op Mine, protesting low wages and poor working conditions. Their protests attracted the attention of United Mine Workers of America (UMWA), AFL-CIO, Catholic relief agencies, and worker advocacy groups like Utahns Against Hunger and Utah Jobs with Justice. The miners' claims are being investigated by the National Labor Relations Board.

Another Kingston business that has attracted much attention is coin-operated amusement machines. According to investigative journalist Lou Kilzer of Denver's *Rocky Mountain News,* the Kingstons have been linked with known organized crime figures in the coin amusement machine business, primarily "New Jersey mob associate, Carmen Ricci" and "Denver's Smaldone La Cosa Nostra syndicate." The principal Kingston amusement coin-operated machine business is Mountain Coin, managed by Eldon Kingston. In an interview with the *Rocky Mountain News,* Eldon denied that they (the Clan) have ever distributed illegal gaming machines or knowingly done business with any organized crime figures. However, Lou Kilzer's February 13, 2000, article is quite convincing.

In 1998 the Kingston Clan grabbed national headlines when John Daniel Kingston was arrested for belt whipping his sixteen-year-old daughter for refusing to live as plural wife number fifteen with her uncle. The uncle, David Ortell Kingston, was arrested for having sex with her. John Daniel was convicted of child abuse and served twenty-eight weeks in jail. David Ortell served four years in prison for incest and was given an unconditional release in June 2003.

According to dissidents from the Kingston Clan, the Kingstons believe their blood is so pure that incest is justified and preferred. They do not seek out new members, and new wives come from inside the group. The Kingston hierarchy, with harems totaling from five to thirty-five wives, get first pick of the girls, which results in not enough girls to supply all the young men in the Clan. Consequently, the less influential young men are forced to go outside the Clan to find wives. The favorite place for the Kingston boys to shop for wives is the AUB (Allred Group) Saturday night dances.

Although they refuse to grant interviews, the Kingstons dominated the news for over two years until, much to their relief, Tom Green grabbed away the spotlight.

The True & Living Church of Jesus Christ of Saints of the Last Days
Unincorporated.
Population: Between 300 - 500
Priesthood leader: James D. Harmston.
The TLC, as it is affectionately called, is unincorporated. The prophet, seer, and revelator is James D. Harmston, who is probably the most innovative and ruthless of all the contemporary Mormon prophets.

The TLC is located at Manti, Utah, a small rural community

in San Pete County in central Utah. (Manti is also the location of the LDS Manti Temple, one of the first temples built by LDS pioneers.)

The media treated polygamy as a harmless lifestyle like the Amish until 1997 and 1998. Jim Harmston took advantage of that misconception and used the media to proselytize and promote his group. He also developed a sophisticated, comprehensive website that attracted many converts.

The TLC evolved from a study group of active Latter-day Saints in San Pete County who were delving into Mormon Fundamentalism. Harmston emerged as the dominate person in the study group and as he assumed and exerted his authority, most of the study group fell away.

The LDS faithful are cautioned by Church authorities to refrain from delving into what is referred to as the "mysteries," which is Mormon Fundamentalism. Harmston, who is inclined to be pugnacious, ignored the admonition and was excommunicated. Soon thereafter, Harmston claimed to have been visited by the Father and the Son and instructed to rebuild the kingdom of God. Jim also claims to be the reincarnation of Joseph Smith and, in that respect, he has attempted to pattern the TLC after the Nauvoo, Illinois, period of Mormon history.

In February 1998 it was leaked to the media that Jim Harmston had married a sixteen-year-old girl. Prior to that he had been photographed numerous times with his eight wives, all older women he had acquired from other polygamist groups.

The media suddenly became interested in Harmston's secret marriage, which marked an end to his courtship with the media. Until then Harmston had been as talkative as Tom Green. He stopped granting interviews and shut down his website. Then in April 1998, Kaziah May Hancock and Cindy Stewart filed a lawsuit against Jim and the TLC.

Harmston was accused of bilking Cindy out of $10,000, and defrauding Kaziah of $250,000. Kaziah's life story, described later in this book, is one of the most tragic to come out of the annals of contemporary Mormon Fundamentalism.

The TLC is one of the smaller groups. Like AUB, the TLC gives the endowment, except Jim goes one step further. He has organized his own version of the Church of the Firstborn. Worthy adherents have their "green" temple apron replaced by a "white" apron.[8]

Harmston has also introduced the doctrine of Multiple Mortal Probation, a form of reincarnation. The TLC patriarch, Phillip Preston Savage, gives each member a patriarchal blessing and in that blessing informs the member who he had been in former lives. Kaziah had been told she was a plural wife of Jesus Christ. Her husband Doug was told he was a brother to Adam. Harmston claims he was not only Joseph Smith, but several other important historical and biblical personalities like Isaiah and King Arthur. After viewing the movie *Braveheart* he suddenly remembered he had been William Wallace.

The TLC also promotes the Doctrine of Rescue, which permits a man with a higher priesthood to take for himself the wife of a man with a lesser priesthood. In 2001 and 2002 Harmston started taking at least one wife from each of his apostles. This caused several of his leading and trusted disciples to apostatize.

The TLC has no corporations or land trusts like the other organized groups. The TLC is financed by tithes and consecrations. In order for a member to be inducted into the Church of the Firstborn, receive a white apron, and have their Calling & Election Made Sure,[9] the member must literally consecrate all of his or her earthly possessions. In this manner several converts have sold their homes and turned the proceeds over to Harmston.

The Righteous Branch of the Church of Jesus Christ of Latter-Day Saints

Unincorporated

Population: Approximately 100

Priesthood leader: Gerald Peterson, Jr.

The Righteous Branch is located at Paiquin, Utah, west of Cedar City. The prophet and leader is Gerald Peterson Jr., who inherited leadership from his father Gerald Peterson Sr. The Petersons claim that the ghost of Rulon Allred appeared to the elder Gerald and gave him all the keys of the kingdom and that Father Adam later appeared to Gerald and ratified Rulon's ordination. All polygamists believe that Adam is the God of this world. When they pray to Heavenly Father, they are praying to Adam.

The Righteous Branch, a small offshoot of the Allred Group (AUB), is relatively unknown and scavenges its members from the other groups. For example, when the TLC started falling apart during the Kaziah May Hancock lawsuit, members of the Righteous Branch encircled Manti like hungry wolves trying to convert TLC dissidents.

Tom Green got his start in the Righteous Branch where he was an apostle. It is not unusual for ambitious fundamentalists like Tom to join an organized group like the Righteous Branch or AUB and use it as a training ground. How long the Righteous Branch will survive is anyone's guess. New groups come and go in the subculture like blisters.

Church of the Firstborn of the Fullness of Times

Incorporated: The Church of the First-born of the Fullness of Times, 9-21-55

Population: About 30 Families

Priesthood leader: Joel LeBaron

In both Mormon and Protestant scriptures, Jesus Christ is identified as the Firstborn. (Romans 13:29) The Mormons tell us that those who are saved unto Christ will become members of the Church of the Firstborn. (D&C 76:53-58) According to the LDS

Church, the Church of the Firstborn is used as a metaphor for the LDS Church. However, dissidents from the LDS Church have formed splinter groups calling themselves the Church of the Firstborn.

The first man to implement and organize the Church of the Firstborn came from the LeBaron family. Ross LeBaron claimed he is the one who did it, others say Alma or Ben LeBaron came up with the idea. But Joel LeBaron gets the credit because it was he who developed a following. Joel founded the community of Los Molinos on the peninsula of Baja, California, in Old Mexico. On September 21, 1955 Joel filed with the State of Utah, "The Church of the Firstborn of the Fullness of Times."

The Church of the Firstborn alleges that Joel received his authority through Benjamin F. Johnson, companion and bodyguard of Joseph Smith. Benjamin allegedly passed the priesthood keys to Alma Dayer LeBaron who allegedly passed them to Joel. The keys, according to the LeBarons, are the *real* patriarchal priesthood keys. They claim these keys are higher, having greater authority than the keys held by the prophet of the LDS Church.

The Church of the Firstborn has been steeped in violence. Ervil LeBaron, Joel's younger brother, challenged Joel's authority. Ervil pulled away from Joel, taking a few fanatics with him, and started the Church of the Lamb of God. Ervil ordered the murder of his brother Joel. He then murdered Rulon C. Allred of the AUB in hopes of luring Verlan M. LeBaron to the funeral so he too could be murdered. In April 1980 Ervil was convicted of ordering the murder of Rulon C. Allred. He died in prison a year later of an alleged heart attack. After Ervil's conviction, Ervil's sons went on carrying out Ervil's death sentences. Before his sons were caught many more were murdered, all in the name of religion.

The motive for the murders was the precious "keys," and the power they believe comes with it. Ervil believed that he was the One Mighty and Strong who it was prophesied would set in order the LDS Church and call to repentance all of mankind. The right of power belonged to him and Ervil set in motion his own sons and wives to assassinate any and all competition to his power and bring down justice on all apostates. It didn't matter that his victims were his brothers, wives, sons, and daughters; when it came to protecting the precious priesthood keys, no one was safe or indispensable.

The Church of the Firstborn is headquartered at Colonia LeBaron in Chihuahua, Mexico. It is still a viable church organization with members scattered throughout Mexico and Texas. But with the death of Ervil LeBaron and the incarceration of his zealot sons, the Church of the Lamb of God dissolved and is no longer a terrorist organization.

While Ervil and his sons were hunting down and killing the opposition, Ross Wesley LeBaron, the oldest of the LeBaron brothers, was back in Utah quietly doing his own thing.

Ross was an eccentric who claimed to be the original brains behind the Church of the Firstborn. He lived in a storage unit with a dirt floor. He believed in flying saucers and was a frequent guest on local radio talk shows. Everyone considered Ross a little crazy, but harmless.

Ross attracted three young disciples, Fred Collier, Tom Green, and Robert Black, who took care of his needs in exchange for tutoring. As insane as he might have been, according to Tom Green, Ross was an encyclopedia of Mormon knowledge and was very convincing in his defense of the patriarchal keys.

After Ross died each of these men, Collier, Green, and Black claimed Ross had passed the keys to him. Each immediately began traveling through the fundamentalist subculture preaching his particular brand of Firstborn Mormonism to anyone who would listen. Of the three, Tom became the most notorious.

Between Green, Collier, and Black there are about thirty families true to the Church of the Firstborn doctrines. Many of these families have left the state, thinking that they too, like Tom, might be prosecuted for bigamy.

Fred Collier

The leaders in all of the organized groups, with the exception of the Kingston Clan, view Collier, Green, and Black as usurpers. Collier, who has published several pamphlets and a historical book promoting Mormon priesthood, was retained by Ortell Kingston before he died in 1987 to teach him the priesthood side of Mormonism. According to Rowenna Erickson, a dissident from the Kingston group and co-founder of Tapestry Against Polygamy, Ortell and his son Paul Kingston literally purchased their priesthood authority from Fred Collier.

In an interview with Collier in 1998 he confirmed that he had indeed taught the Kingstons for money, and that he had also taught Owen Allred and James D. Harmston many important priesthood truths that Harmston and Allred pretended they had obtained by divine inspiration. Collier obtained his esoteric information by stealing it from the LDS Church archives with Tom Green as his accomplice.

When Tom and Fred Collier were teamed up as the acolytes of Ross LeBaron, they had a genealogy friend who gave them access to the LDS Church archives. Tom confided to me that he and Collier's wife Bonnie would smuggle microfilm out of the archives to Collier. Bonnie put the microfilm in her bra and Tom hid microfilm in his shorts. Collier would make copies of the microfilm, then Tom and Bonnie would smuggle the microfilm back into the archives. I later confirmed the story during an interview with Collier.

The microfilm consisted of journals, sermons, and biographies of nineteenth-century Mormon leaders. Tom didn't feel like it was stealing. In his mind he was merely rescuing important information that all of Mormondom was entitled too.

Independent Mormon Fundamentalists

There may be as many as a 1000 families practicing plural marriage who are not associated with an organized group. These families are referred to as Independents. According to the

Independents, Lorin Woolley said, "Don't organize!" He cautioned the polygamists against organizing in competition with the LDS Church or doing anything that would attract attention.

Ogden Kraut, a respected independent fundamentalist, historian, and author confided in a tape recorded interview shortly before he died that he was convinced there were as many as 100,000 independent polygamists.

Ogden is the author of dozens of pamphlets and books dealing with Mormon Fundamentalism. Because of his writings he was looked upon as the unofficial patriarch of the Independents. Ogden was my friend and I respected his judgement, but in this case, although his intentions are well meaning, I believe his estimate is grossly exaggerated; there is simply no evidence to support his hypothesis.

If there was anyone who totally believed in the divinity of The Church of Jesus Christ of Latter-day Saints and plural marriage, it was Ogden Kraut. His entire life was devoted to the authentication of Mormonism and the principle of plural marriage. For him there was no greater cause, no higher calling, and so he thought that there were thousands of dedicated Mormons like himself, still active members of the LDS Church, living celestial marriage in secret. However, Ogden also thought that Chinese militants were massing on the borders of Mexico ready to invade the United States.

The Independent polygamist families gather in informal groups to do their worshiping. Each head of family is entitled to revelation for his family. As a rule they represent no threat to society, except that there can be abuse to women and children as Vicki Prunty of Tapestry Against Polygamy can testify. Vickie once belonged to an independent family.

The Christian Polygamists

The Mormons are not the only Christians who have resurrected plural marriage from the Old Testament. There are dozens, perhaps hundreds of Christian polygamist families throughout the United States. The most visible Christian polygamist is Steve Butt, who started Broken Shackles Ministry, an escape network for abused women.

Steve is a dissident from Jehovah's Witness, which he declared was an oppressive religious organization. As he searched the Bible for a religious cure to the mental and emotional ills suffered by victims of oppressive cults, he was intrigued by the plural marriages of the ancient prophets. One thing led to another and he wound up taking as a plural wife an abused woman he was helping.

Steve felt that the Mormons were giving plural marriage a bad name by making plural marriage a doctrine and commandment. He said he had found nothing in the Bible to support the Mormon hypophysis that plural marriage was a commandment. For Steve, plural marriage was not a religious tenet but a custom, a social unit or alternative form of marriage practiced by Abraham and the early Christians. It had nothing to do with heaven or exaltation, and was strictly an earthly practice.

In spite of this altruistic approach to plural marriage, Steve's ministry began to focus on the benefits of plural marriage, for women as well as men. He moved from New England to Utah in about 1996 and put together an Internet website called Broken Shackles Ministry and Bfree.org.

His website attracted dozens of men and women who felt as he did. As a result, his ministry turned into an Internet ministry. Before long Steve was in competition with Tom Green as a talk show guest. In fact, they appeared together on the Queen Latifah Show, March 27, 2001.

Steve purchased a vacant former LDS church building in the small Mormon community of Circleville, Utah, the hometown of outlaw Butch Cassidy. At first the Circleville natives were shocked when they learned that Steve was a polygamist pastor who had made their little town his headquarters. But gradually things calmed down when it became obvious that Steve was not a threat to their lifestyle or community.

All seemed to be going well for Steve. A third wife joined his family. Converts began to move to Circleville, and donations were filtering in. He was at the apogee of his ministry when things began to nosedive. He learned that one of his converts had been molesting his daughter and he quickly reported the man to the local sheriff. Then contentions developed among his followers, and worst of all contentions in his own family.

Steve sold the church building and moved to Washington State. More family problems developed as one wife left him and another threatened to leave. His polygamy misadventure had turned into a nightmare.

Steve is now relocated in Texas. A deeply religious man, he still has his ministry, but now the focus is on Jesus Christ and not plural marriage.

Chapter Three

Anti-polygamy and Pro-polygamy Movements

Tapestry Against Polygamy

Tapestry Against Polygamy made its debut in Salt Lake City in 1998. A non-profit organization, it advocates against the human right violations inherent in polygamy and provides assistance to individuals leaving polygamous cults.

It was begun by former plural wives who had escaped from their polygamist shackles. The women came from every polygamist group in Utah and Arizona and one activist, Carmen Thompson, came from a Christian (non-Mormon) polygamist group. Over the years, some of the activists have dropped out of Tapestry or moved away, but still remain viable opponents of polygamy.

Co-founders Vicky Prunty and Rowenna Erickson remain the most visible. Vicky was a plural wife in an independent family. Rowenna was a plural wife in the infamous Kingston Clan. Consequently, she quickly became the most sought after source for information about the Kingstons.

As Tom Green became more and more notorious as a pro-polygamy guest on television talk shows, the women from Tapestry were matched against Tom. As a result they appeared on the same talk shows and there developed a deep-seated enmity between Tapestry and Tom, and polygamists in general.

Due to the circus atmosphere orchestrated by a few television producers, Tapestry became more selective before they would appear as guests. But not Tom, he relished the limelight and would talk anywhere, anytime, anyplace. You will read more about these women throughout this book.

Learn more: http://www.polygamy.org/

Help The Child Brides

Help The Child Brides is a non-profit, political movement dedicated to combating alleged child abuses occurring in the FLDS religious group that dominates the twin cities of Hildale, Utah, and Colorado City, Arizona. In October, 2002, Bob Curran, who organized the movement, opened an office on Tabernacle Street in downtown St. George, Utah.

Help The Child Brides has been doing in Southern Utah what Tapestry has been doing in Northern Utah – making government and the media aware of the criminal behavior in organized polygamist groups. Bob Curran and dissident women from the FLDS deserve well earned credit in bringing together the Attorneys General of Utah and Arizona in a common effort to combat the abuse in the FLDS.

Many moving and informative stories are contained on their website, some written by women, others by newspaper reporters. Learn more: www.helpthechildbrides.com

Women's Religious Liberties Union, WRLU

Friday, July 31, 1998, Utahn Mary Potter held a news conference and announced that she was heading a new women's group that advocated polygamy as a political right. Their goal was to overturn laws that prohibited polygamy. The movement was obviously inspired to oppose Tapestry Against Polygamy.

At the time, Mary Potter was the sole wife of Roy Potter, the Murray City Policeman who was fired in 1982 when it was discovered he had three wives.

A few plural wives among the independents, Tom Green's wives, and a few more from AUB rallied around Mary. The pro-polygamy women held a few rallies, demonstrated in front of *The Salt Lake Tribune* building and marched up and down in front of

Tapestry's headquarters. But when Mary and Roy experienced marital difficulties, Mary dropped the ball and no one else picked up the pieces. The WRLU has since been lost to history.

Mormon Focus

Since the withdrawal of Mary Potter and the WRLU, the pro-polygamy crowd was hurting for someone to take up the banner. The adverse publicity sparked by the prosecution of Tom Green had driven most polygamists further underground. The media was hard-pressed for someone other than Tom Green who was willing to speak out and come to the defense of plural marriage.

After the publication of my first fact-based novel *Murder of a Prophet,* which focused on the dark side of Mormon Fundamentalism, two plural wives and a former plural wife took it upon themselves to become the pro-polygamy vanguard. According to informants close to the three talented ladies, the non-fiction book *Voices In Harmony* was created and published to offset the damage they felt I had done to the sacred principle of plural marriage.

The three intrepid ladies earned media recognition consistent with their advocacy and, as a result, two of the ladies became the unofficial spokeswomen for the advancement and preservation of plural marriage.

One of the ladies, Anne Wilde, the widowed plural wife of Ogden Kraut, teamed up with author Shane I. Whelan and published *Mormon Focus,* an apologetic magazine defending plural marriage. The magazine in every respect is well done and in good form, and it has the potential of becoming the official voice of Mormon Fundamentalism. However, the first issue published in October 2003 focuses on just the bright side of plural marriage and ignores the FLDS and Kingston abuses that are routinely reported by Utah and Arizona newspapers.

Mary Batchelor, co-author of *Voices In Harmony,* has gradually emerged as the principle face and spokeswoman of the plural marriage advocates. According to reliable sources she helped organize a "by invitation only" meeting between plural wives of

Centennial Park and Utah Attorney General Mark Shurtleff. Mary's advocacy makes for an interesting scenario because Mary and Vicky Prunty (of Tapestry Against Polygamy) are former sister wives, the plural wives of Gary Batchelor, who is the copy editor of *Mormon Focus.*

Mormon Fundamentalism today has all the ingredients of a good story: intrigue, sex, power, plunder, deception, money, murder, and a potpourri of fascinating, macabre characters. It also has in place all the esoteric ingredients with which to form a cult: supernatural direction, doctrine, structure, and purpose.

Overall, Latter-day Saints are a great people and loyal Americans. The LDS Church is a virtuous, safe place to raise children. Unfortunately, unprincipled men resurrect doctrines that are better left in the past. Early Mormon doctrine in the hands of a diabolical or deluded personality can be as dangerous as whiskey to a drunk driver, creating zealot unpredictability. Brian David Mitchell, the fanatic who kidnaped Elizabeth Smart, is a classic example.

Pro-polygamy advocates maintain that plural marriage is about families. This is true, partially ... a few polygamist families do seem to portray a paradigm of family cohesiveness. But overall, especially in the organized groups, I will show that plural marriage is about power, sex, and money – that "power" overshadows and in some cases obliterates the "love" in plural relationships. And I will show how combating abuse among polygamists is complicated by the First Amendment to the U.S. Constitution, which states in part: Congress shall make no law respecting an establishment of religion, or prohibiting the free exercise thereof.

Nevertheless, I will also show that the governments of Utah and Arizona are taking positive steps towards protecting the civil rights of men, women, and children trapped in polygamist relationships.

Chapter Four

An Inside Look at AUB Fraud

Virginia Hill's lawsuit against Owen A. Allred et. al. filed in August 1997, and then the 1998 arrest of John Daniel Kingston for belt whipping his sixteen-year-old daughter, and David Ortell Kingston's conviction for having sex with her were the pivotal points where the media started reporting the corrupt side of Mormon Fundamentalism.

Prior to 1997, there had been incidents of violence, but they were treated more as anomalies rather than as inherent characteristics of the underground lifestyle. The media was unaware of the sexual abuse, welfare fraud, and other forms of corruption that were perpetrated on a regular basis in the secret enclaves of organized Fundamentalism. At last, the truth was coming out.

The violence prior to 1997 can be quickly summarized. In 1977, Dr. Rulon C. Allred was murdered by Ervil LeBaron. In 1977, John Singer was shot and killed by a deputy sheriff for resisting arrest. Ervil was captured in 1980, convicted of the Allred murder and died of a heart attack in the Utah State Prison the following year. In 1984, Ron and Dan Lafferty cut the throats of their sister-in-law and her sixteen-month-old daughter. In 1988, Adam Swapp and his brothers, in retaliation of John Singer's killing, bombed an LDS chapel in Kamas, Utah. In the thirteen day standoff that followed, one peace officer was killed. In the nine years that followed these crimes, the media treated Utah polygamy as an eccentric, but harmless way of life, discounting the previous violence as uncommon.

For example, on February 23, 1992, *The Salt Lake Tribune* published a three-page feature story about Apostolic United Brethren and included Owen Allred's photograph. In the same article was a photograph of middle-aged Dennis E. Matthews with his five pretty wives and sixteen adorable children, all depicted as the ideal polygamous family. This was the pinnacle point in Matthews' adventure into plural marriage, when he was on top of the polygamous world. He was a coveted member of Owen Allred's inner circle. He had access to plenty of money, a respectable job with a fireworks company, and a mansion-sized house in Mapleton, Utah. Matthews was a key player in the Virginia Hill lawsuit. Today, he has only one wife, he works at odd jobs, and he is a million dollars in debt.

Who is Virginia Hill? She's a buxom redhead born Marsha Jones in Southern Utah, but raised in Las Vegas. At age eighteen, looking like she was twenty-one, Marsha was dancing in a chorus line in one of the most popular casinos on Las Vegas' famous strip.

Marsha was right at home in the bright lights and excitement of the gaming industry. Confident and capable, like many other beautiful young girls who were caught up in the glamour of Las Vegas, she changed her name to Virginia Hill in honor of her mentor, the paramour of New York gangster Benjamin "Bugsy" Siegel.[10] Bugsy is the man who built the famous Flamingo Casio and brought the "mob" to Las Vegas. It was the mob's investment that put Las Vegas on the map.

After legally changing her name, Virginia's life was not quite as wild, but just as interesting as her mentor's life. Because of her natural beauty and charm, Virginia was always welcome in the casinos where she, as often as not, brought luck to high rollers. If she brought luck, it was customary to tip the lucky lady. Virginia had a shoe box on her closet shelf and, when it was full, she would deposit as much as $75,000 in the bank. On two occasions, her benefactor, a frequent visitor to Las Vegas, was a redheaded gentleman who fought fires around the world. They called him Red Adair.

In the 1970s she was labeled as the Sex Symbol of Las Vegas. She not only danced but sang and acted in a couple of South American movies. Under the able management of Rolando Larraz, she owned a Las Vegas weekly newspaper *LaVerdad* (The Truth), and a Spanish television show *El Show Del Mediodia* (The Afternoon Show). In 1977 Virginia put together a show at the Barcelona Hotel entitled *She's A Lady,* a tribute to singer Tom Jones. At one point in her career she was forced to hire three bodyguards to discourage unwanted male suitors. According to Larraz, it was not unusual for Virginia to walk around with as much as $80,000 dollars in cash. In just one night, according to Larraz, she came home with $100,000. Those were exciting days when the dollar slots took real silver dollars and before the United States became a cashless society.

From Las Vegas, Virginia moved to Miami where she became the mistress of multimillionaire Jim Bergen. According to her manager Rolando Larraz, Virginia lived on the second floor of the Biscayne Terrace Hotel for two years where she owned and managed Virginia Hill Boutique. The relationship had a friendly ending. She walked away with two million dollars.

In 1983 Virginia married Harry Allen Hilf, who Detroit newspapers dubbed the Godfather of Detroit Gambling. Harry, like Bugsy, was Jewish and Virginia converted to Judaism.

Virginia was happily married to Harry. She was faithful and domesticated. They traveled between Las Vegas, Detroit, and Miami. They met and associated with people of rank, power, money, and position, some names of which would be easily recognizable. It was a world of bright lights, champaign, caviar, and exotic furs. The common denominator between Harry, Virginia, and their celebrity friends was wealth, prestige, and power. But in 1987 Camelot was about to come to an end. Agents of the Federal Bureau of Investigation were authorized to intercept wire communications and conduct telephone transmission interceptions on Harry Allen Hilf and several other men they identified as being part of the Detroit La Cosa Nostra (LCN) family.

According to an FBI report in 1963, a United States Senate Permanent Subcommittee on Investigations of the Committee on Government Operation into organized crime (chaired by Senator John L. McClellan) identified a Detroit La Cosa Nostra (LDCN) Mafia blood and marriage family, as controlling and engaging in rackets involving narcotics trafficking, prostitution, loansharking, labor racketeering, extortion, and gambling. The report indicated that the "big money" came from gambling, because of all the rackets, it yielded the "highest profit" at the "lowest risk."

FBI surveillance over the years were used to develop probable cause for the wire and telephone interceptions. Cited in the FBI's affidavit of probable cause was an LCN executive meeting in 1979, at the Timberland Game Ranch in Dexter Township, Michigan, in which "Black Bill" Rocco's son Jack was allegedly elected the new boss. Harry, who like Bugsy had a Jewish heritage, was not named among the LCN hierarchy, but the seventy-nine page affidavit did profile him as a close associate with an infamous past.[11] To make matters worse, Virginia found out that Harry had been unfaithful. He had a mistress on the side.

Harry was accused by the United States Government of racketeering, money laundering, and income tax evasion. In 1990, Harry worked out a deal with the United States Attorney, entered a plea, and went to prison.

Between Harry's unfaithfulness and the FBI intrusions,[12] Virginia was devastated and it affected her health. In 1989 she spent several depressive weeks in bed under a doctor's care before she was able to find a possible solution to her dilemma. She concluded that her marriage to Harry was irreconcilable. The IRS and FBI were moving in. She had to separate her assets from Harry as soon as possible or the government agents would seize her assets along with his. Once that happened she knew it would take years of legal haggling to recover her assets from the government.

There was a spiritual side to Virginia. While Harry was doing business in Miami, she might be found tanning on a beach and reading the Bible. It was this spiritual side that contributed to her decision to make a major change in her life. Although traumatized and under a doctor's care, she resolved to divorce Harry and move to St. George, Utah, to be near her mother, Connie Jones.

Connie had a sister, Lola, who was married to Danny Jackson, one of those rare individuals of exceptional honesty. Danny was also an extraordinarily devoted man who believed in Mormon Fundamentalism and had closely explored but not joined the AUB. Danny and Lola lived in the quaint, village-like town of Santa Clara, ten miles southwest of St. George.

Danny's best friend and spiritual leader was a charismatic former Mormon, now fundamentalist, by the name of John Shugart. Both Danny and John Shugart had been raised in Las Vegas. Consequently, they did not view gambling as a sin but an industry. Shugart had inherited one fifth of the Showboat Casino, which he promptly sold for a million dollars and eventually squandered.

On September 17, 1989, knowing it was coming, Uncle Danny Jackson received a UPS package wrapped with brown paper. It was postmarked, Virginia Hill, Detroit, Michigan. Inside the package were neatly packed bundles of greenbacks in $50 and $100 denominations. Each bundle contained $10,000. The combined bundles totaled $200,000. Virginia was trying to protect her assets and apparently felt her money would be best protected in cash.

In the next four weeks, Uncle Danny received two more packages containing currency. The cash received in the three packages totaled 1.2 million dollars, all legal tender, all sent UPS, and all from his niece Virginia Hill.

Sending cash via UPS sounds like a strange way to handle money, but it is not something new. The Chicago and New York crime families did it all the time.

It took three months for Virginia to settle her affairs before she completed her move to St. George. In the meantime, Danny felt the currency was unsafe in his house because of all the kids coming and going. Danny's friend and spiritual leader, John Shugart, the man

Danny trusted more than life itself, offered to keep the money in his house.

Virginia was impressed with Shugart and trusted him because her mother and Uncle Danny trusted him. She attended a few of Shugart's spiritual meetings and found it refreshing to be among people who, she thought, put spirituality over earthly things like sex and money. She was impressed with Danny and Shugart's morality and their apparent desire to serve the Lord and live an exemplary life. She thought John Shugart was a man who practiced what he preached and she had no problem with him holding her money in trust.

As it turned out, Virginia could handle herself in the world of gamblers and gangsters, but she was totally fooled by the outward piety of Fundamentalists. What she didn't know is that John Shugart had been obsessed with possessing the notorious Desert Inn Ranch, the one time hideout and recreational ranch of the Las Vegas mob. As luck would have it, Virginia was planning to purchase a ranch, a quiet secluded place away from the noise and frantic pace of the city. So let's examine these spiritual men and their motives.

John Shugart was a dissident member of Apostolic United Brethren. He was an intelligent, well-read man who wanted to start up his own fundamentalist group. Shugart claimed to be receiving and recording revelations that he felt were as sophisticated as the ones received by Joseph Smith. Danny was his loyal acolyte and believed Shugart was divinely inspired or possibly, Joseph Smith reincarnated.

Previously, John Shugart had entered the Allred Group (AUB). With his silver tongue, pious demeanor, and knowledge of Mormonism, he worked his way into the AUB hierarchy and was made a bishop at Pinesdale, Montana. Shugart was like a lot of other converts in AUB, a "rainbow chaser" looking for the proverbial pot of gold, a wheeler and dealer with a big money-making scheme just on the horizon, believing all the while that God would bless him in special and huge ways. Owen A. Allred, the prophet and leader of AUB, also had an eye for an easy fast buck and had gathered around him in his priesthood inner circle, ambitious, godly men of dubious scruples. Before long, Shugart and Allred established a close ecclesiastic and fiduciary relationship.

In 1979, two years after the murder of Rulon C. Allred, Shugart inveigled Owen into going into partnership with him in the purchase of the Desert Inn Ranch, commonly referred to as the DI. A contract was drawn up, but as it turned out, Shugart and Owen both had ulterior motives. Shugart thought he could use AUB to eventually possess the ranch for himself, and Owen thought he could use Shugart to enrich AUB with one more ranch. Inasmuch as AUB was a sole corporation of the Presiding Elder, whatever AUB owned, so did Owen A. Allred.

AUB took possession that same year and moved a few families onto the ranch with John Shugart in charge. The DI was eventually lost and Shugart and Owen blamed each other. It is unknown how much money Shugart lost; he allegedly had sold his house for $150,000 and used it as down payment. AUB lost $100,000. It was a misadventure for which Owen Allred would never forgive Shugart, nor would he forget.

Shugart's and Allred's Desert Inn Escapade

Six separate "Contract and Declarations of Trust" deeds were executed by the AUB in the country of Belize and under the laws of Belize to finance the DI Ranch. They were: Pinesdale Investment, Midway Trust Co., Bitterroot Investment, Clear Water Co., South West Farms, and Desert Inn Ranch.[13] All of the deeds are dated, December 2, 1979.

Belize is a Caribbean country bounded on the north by Mexico and on the south and west by Guatemala. Belize received its independence from the United Kingdom September 21, 1981. Guatemala would not recognize Belize until 1992. A country about the size of Massachusetts, Belize has been plagued with the South American drug trade, illicit banking and money laundering, high unemployment, and urbane crime. Back in the 1980s Belize did not have a good reputation.

When AUB took on the DI Ranch, big things were expected – green houses, vineyards, a place of refuge from world catastrophes. John Shugart preached that nearby Sand Valley was a holy place where a treasure was hidden under a big rock and that ghosts of the ancient Nephites (a group of people from The Book of Mormon) traipsed the valley at night. He also taught that Sand Valley was a hideout for the Gadianton Robbers.[14] John used revelations to manipulate people into doing his bidding.

According to Danny Jackson, Owen Allred threw a big dedicatory barbecue celebrating the expected purchase of the DI Ranch. A kid's foot race was organized to keep the children busy. The men, moved by the spirit, bore their testimonies in deference to God's help in obtaining the wonderful DI Ranch.

The DI Ranch, formerly the Las Vegas mob's recreational ranch, was located in a large ravine carved out by the East Fork of Beaver Dam Creek, about sixteen miles west of Santa Clara, and five miles east of Motoqua, an AUB settlement located on the West Fork of Beaver Dam Creek. There was a large rambling ranch house, a fancy stable with sixteen stalls, a barn, and other structures incidental to a ranch. The DI was located in an extremely secluded and beautiful location in Southern Utah, but self-sufficient it was not. There was not enough arable land and water to support itself as a working ranch.

Hidden among the junipers on top of the rim of the ravine was a short landing strip barely large enough for a small plane. Gossip among the AUB polygamists was replete with stories – the landing strip was used to smuggle illegal drugs, dead bodies were buried in the underbrush, and stool-pigeons were tortured in the basement of the ranch house, none of which could be confirmed.

After all the celebrating, the DI Ranch deal fell through because of financial bungling, and Shugart and Owen Allred became bitter enemies, each blaming the other. The owner of the ranch, Herb Fletcher, became thoroughly disgusted with both Allred and Shugart, especially Shugart. The reason the DI was lost is steeped in accusations of deception and dishonesty by all parties.

Nevertheless, Shugart did not recover from his obsession to possess the DI Ranch and saw in Virginia one more chance.

Shugart talked Virginia into purchasing the DI Ranch and in October 1989 arranged for his good and trusted friend Dennis E. Matthews to show Virginia the DI on two separate occasions. Shugart was afraid that if Herb Fletcher knew he was involved in the purchase, he wouldn't sell. During that time, Virginia was busy commuting back and forth to Detroit and authorized Shugart to arrange for the purchase.

Dennis Matthews was a member of AUB in good standing and kept up a close relationship with Shugart, who was trying to woo Matthews away from Owen Allred. Shugart led Matthews to believe that the DI Ranch would be a place of refuge[15] and under Matthews control. He wanted to make Dennis the bishop over the DI. The two would spend hours into the wee night talking gospel. Shugart thought they must have been best friends before they were born.

Matthews convinced Shugart that he did not have the expertise to negotiate the purchase, Fletcher was a tough customer, and there were so many things to consider, water rights, BLM grazing rights, etc. But he had a friend named John C. Putvin, a hotshot realtor who was a crackerjack negotiator. For $40,000 Putvin would put together the deal.

On November 12, 1989, Virginia, Shugart, Uncle Danny, Dennis Matthews, and John C. Putvin met in Shugart's Santa Clara home. A million dollars in cash was counted out on the kitchen table. Matthews wanted the kitchen curtains pulled so nobody could look in. Shugart laughed and asked, "Why? The money is perfectly legal."

Putvin, who sported dark glasses with an unlit cigar in his mouth, explained that Fletcher would not accept cash. Putvin, nonchalant and apparently unimpressed by the large amounts of cash, proposed an alternate plan. He knew of people with good business sense where they could invest the money short term, reclaim it with interest in a negotiable form acceptable to Fletcher.

John Putvin is an excellent, charismatic salesman. He was able to sell himself as an honest man to Virginia and Shugart. At the time he, like Matthews, was a polygamist and about to enter the inner circle of Owen A. Allred. Matthews had convinced Shugart that Putvin's reputation and integrity was impeccable. What he didn't tell Shugart is that Putvin had recently lost his realtor's license due to equity skimming. Nor did he tell Shugart of Putvin's cloak and dagger paranoia, Putvin's shell corporations, and many phony addresses.

Shugart and Virginia agreed to Putvin's plan, providing Dennis Matthews, whom Shugart trusted implicitly, kept track of the money, where it went, names, account numbers, etc. There was no written contract. After all, Matthews and Shugart were brothers in the priesthood, where a man's word was more binding than a piece of paper.

Under cover of darkness, Shugart, Jackson, Matthews, and Putvin went to a St. George storage shed used as a home storage canning facility. While Putvin kept an eye out for intruders, the other three placed one million dollars in several gallon cans, pouring wheat over the currency, and then sealing the cans. Putvin didn't want to take the chance of being stopped by a State Trooper and then trying to explain the currency. The million dollars represented the first installment. The purchase price of the ranch was 1.5 million. Putvin had been given his $40,000 fee in advance.

According to Matthews' later testimony, they had no sooner left St. George on their way back to Salt Lake City, when Putvin said, "We're not giving the money back." Matthews claimed they argued and finally decided to go see their priesthood leader Owen Allred, the following day.

On November 13, 1989, Owen Allred, Matthews, and Putvin met at Allred's Bluffdale, Utah, home. Owen was in the habit of tape recording important priesthood business, therefore, the conversation was tape recorded.

Putvin did most of the talking. He explained that a born again Christian women, for whatever reason, had donated to John Shugart a large sum of money. Putvin and Matthews knew that Owen still had a deep-seated hatred for Shugart and wanted Owen to think that the money belonged to Shugart. Putvin said that Matthews had been given one million dollars to purchase the DI Ranch.

When Owen heard, "million dollars," he said, "That's what John Shugart cheated us out of." With excitement in his voice, Matthews confirmed to Owen that he had in his possession, one million dollars.

Putvin explained that he was afraid if Shugart was allowed to purchase the DI, "he would be in a position to hurt our people," meaning the AUB people living at Motoqua. After considerable exchange of comments, mostly referring to the wickedness of John Shugart, Putvin and Matthews asked Owen to inquire of the Lord what they should do with the money. Putvin suggested they could purchase the DI and put it in Dennis Matthew's name. Owen asked Dennis, "But what if Shugart wanted you to sign it back over to him?" Dennis said he would do it, unless he (Owen) told him different. After a few seconds of hesitation, Owen said, "Get title to the Granite and get title to the DI, and tell nobody."

In the meantime, Danny Jackson, John Shugart, and Shugart's son Johnny flew to Detroit where they met Virginia. They purchased a sledgehammer and crowbar and used it to recover 2.2 million dollars in cash hidden beneath the cement floor of the garage. Virginia then purchased a new Jeep and, at Shugart's suggestion, put it in John Shugart's name so Virginia's estranged husband couldn't claim it. Danny drove Virginia's Cadillac with the 2.2 million in the trunk, while Shugart and his son followed in the Jeep. Two days later they were back in Santa Clara. A few days after that, Dennis Matthews, driving a new Honda, showed up to see Virginia and pick up the final half million dollars to complete the purchase of the DI.

Owen Allred then gave John Putvin and Dennis Matthews ecclesiastical blessings from on high. The following day, Owen ordained Matthews bishop over the DI Ranch.

Once Owen Allred entered the picture, things moved fast, but Putvin was in the driver's seat. John Putvin, Dennis Matthews, J. LaMoine Jenson, Paul Hess, and Owen A. Allred jumped into Owen's suburban and drove to St. George where they inspected the DI Ranch.[16]

Suddenly they decided *not* to purchase the DI Ranch. They already had the Granite Ranch, they reasoned, so they would pay it off and *have money left over.*

On November 20, 1989, Owen A. Allred and his son Glen Allred negotiated with Moench Investment Company, LTD, the seller of the Granite, and paid off the unpaid balance. The ranch immediately became the property of Red Cedar Corporation.[17]

The Granite Ranch is a multimillion dollar dairy ranch located in Juab County near the Nevada-Utah border in what is called Snake Valley. The nearest town of any size, Delta, Utah, is 125 miles away, most of which is graveled road. Glen Allred manages the Granite. How Owen and Glen obtained the Granite is a unique story in itself. Glen is the only owner known to have put his own money in the ranch, which is a drop in the bucket compared to the tithing money and other donated money from gullible AUB members, who were told they were helping to build the kingdom of God.[18]

In the meantime, John Shugart, Danny Jackson, and Virginia Hill attempted to obtain information from Dennis Matthews about the investment of buying the Desert Inn Ranch, but Matthews was evasive. Finally, they caught Matthews at his office in South Salt Lake. Matthews told them that Putvin ran off with "every red cent" and he had no idea where Putvin could be found.

On March 10, 1990, Virginia, Shugart, and Jackson visited Owen A. Allred. The meeting was arranged by a friend, Ogden Kraut, who was present during the meeting. Irritated by Shugart's presence, Owen held his temper. Shugart explained that John Putvin had disappeared with money that belonged to Virginia, money that was supposed to buy the DI Ranch, and asked his help in locating Putvin.

Up to this point Owen had been under the impression that Virginia had *donated* the money to Shugart. Knowing the truth, he could have taken steps to have the money returned to Virginia, but he chose to deny any knowledge of the money, nor did he know the whereabouts of John Putvin. Owen assured her that neither he nor Dennis Matthews had anything to do with the loss of her money.

In 1994, Owen told the author on three different occasions that two men brought a box filled with currency and put it in the closet of his wife Vera. He couldn't remember who the men were. Finally, on the morning of December 7, 1994, he remembered the two men were Dennis Matthews and John Putvin. In all probability the money was in Vera's closet, not fifteen feet away, when Virginia asked Owen for help.

On March 10, 1990, acting on the recommendation of John Shugart, Virginia hired Roy Potter, former Murray City Policeman, to hunt down Putvin, but Putvin had covered his tracks with false addresses and fictitious names.

Virginia Hill filed a lawsuit against Owen Allred et al. Rod Williams (former uniformed officer for the Secret Service during the Nixon years, and then Border Patrol officer) and I took over the investigation and learned all the intricate details of what happened. All that transpired as years passed would make an entire book in itself. The complexity of following the money was quite an education for me. The intricacy with which the money was transferred from person to person, hidden in various accounts, etc, was fascinating to me as a former law enforcement officer. Even money laundering charges were brought against some of the participants.

In March 6, 2003, *The Salt Lake Tribune* headline read: "Polygamists Lose in Court."
By Kevin Cantera. Kevin's opening statement couldn't have been said better:

> "Polygamous leader Owen Allred laundered thousands of dollars in cash, and his church – the Apostolic United Brethren (AUB) – conspired to steal thousands more, a judge has ruled in a multimillion-dollar lawsuit."

Suffice it to say, what happened is not unusual. Justifying what they do as "God's work," the Fundamentalists believe they can operate outside the law. The story of Virginia Hill is only one story of many.

Chapter Five

An Inside Look at TLC Fraud

While we waited for the Utah Supreme Court to rule on the Virginia Hill case, other polygamists throughout Utah were making news. In early March 1998 I received a telephone call from Don Redd, the attorney for Virginia Hill, asking if I would be interested in becoming the investigator in a lawsuit against another polygamist group, The True & Living Church of Jesus Christ of Saints of the Last Days (TLC), headquartered in Manti, Utah.

The plaintiff's were Kaziah May Hancock and Cindy Stewart, two dissident members of the TLC. When Kaziah and Cindy read about the Virginia Hill lawsuit they went to see Don Redd, who took their case more out of compassion for the two women than anything else.

The TLC is the alter ego of its founder James D. Harmston, a stocky chunk of a man in his early sixties. Urged on by his bitterness against the LDS Church, Harmston began giving a series of classes called "the models," which attracted Mormon Fundamentalists from other groups. On November 25, 1990, he claimed to have been visited by four angels – Enoch, Noah, Abraham, and Moses – who ceremoniously took the priesthood keys from the LDS Church and gave them to him. From that enigmatic beginning, the unincorporated TLC grew to a population of three to five hundred.

Kaziah May Hancock, age forty, drove to my Salt Lake County home from Manti for the initial interview. She was wearing a brown cowboy hat with a rooster feather, and an ankle length western, leather coat. She was rustic and rural in dress, manners and speech, a truly extraordinary lady.

When Kaziah began her story she started to sob uncontrollably. It was forty-five minutes before she could regain control long enough for me to piece together her story. The venting was therapeutic. It was the first time since dissenting from the TLC that she could release pent-up emotions.

Kaziah was born and raised in the FLDS on a small isolated farm on the Arizona Strip south of Colorado City. When Kaziah was age fifteen, Guy Musser, a priesthood leader in the FLDS, gave her as a plural wife to a man old enough to be her grandpa. As a plural wife she was nothing more than maid servant and sex object.

The plural family moved to West Jordan, Utah, where they operated Reclaim Barrel, a company that restored and resold metal barrels. As Kaziah matured she was unable to bear children, so she devoted herself to building up the family business. Kaziah worked alongside the men, lifting and welding, and built the business into profitable enterprise.

For thirteen years she worked like a man and became the sole support of her older husband and two sister-wives, except for welfare. Kaziah said the business grew and prospered and was put in her name so she could handle the business end of things. The middle wife bore children, but for Social Security purposes, the first wife was recorded on birth certificates as the mother. The first wife then divorced the husband and went on welfare.

When Kaziah left the relationship, the husband James Reed Stratton sued Kaziah stating that the reason the business was put in Kaziah's name was so she could provide for him and the other two wives for the rest of their lives. But because Kaziah was the only one who worked the business, the court affirmed that the business belonged to Kaziah.

After a bitter divorce, she sold the business and moved to Indianola in San Pete County where she purchased sixty-seven acres and built a $120,000 log house. Indianola was the bright spot of her life. She loved goats and before long had a small heard of blooded goats with a few sheep and calves thrown in.

Kaziah began taking art lessons at Salt Lake County Community College and fell in love with her art teacher, Ivan Douglas Jordan. Doug became a disciple of James Harmston who sealed Kaziah to Doug in a spiritual wedding. Harmston made Doug an apostle and placed him in charge of the law of consecration, which he took very seriously. Doug climbed to the top of a mountain where he fasted and prayed until he received a revelation dictating how the TLC should administer consecrations. Doug wrote the revelation on scraps of paper. The law of consecration as taught by Joseph Smith is a commandment that instructs members to consecrate their time, energy, and earthly possessions to God's church (which is controlled by the prophet).

Doug moved in with Kaziah but became sullen and moody because he felt like a hired hand. Kaziah loved Doug and alleviated his feelings of inadequacy by legally marrying him and deeding him half ownership of her property.

Doug became deathly sick and Harmston, who was revered as a prophet, was summoned to administer to Doug. Upon arrival at the Indianola property, Harmston claimed to witness several devils battling a couple of angels who were guarding the house. He told Kaziah and Doug the devils were the cause of the sickness and that Indianola was outside the Holy Shekinah, an imaginary protective circle. He advised them to sell out and move to the protection of Manti, which Harmston claimed was the center of Zion. It took a bit of research to discover the meaning of Shekinah.

According to a website called Shekinah, the following is explained: It is a Hebrew word meaning the "presence of God" and refers to the feminine side of the holy spirit. It was believed that the Shekinah "descended in pillar of smoke and guided the Israelites across the desert as a protective presence."

Shekinah is also associated with Hieros Gamos, a Greek term that means sacred marriage or spiritual act. According to another website, www.lindahinks.com: "... early Jewish tradition involved ritualistic sex in the Temple, the belief being that the Holy of Holies in Solomon's Temple housed not only god but his powerful female equal, Shekinah."

The lindahinks website went on to say: "Historically, ritual sex was the act through which male and female experienced God. It was believed that through physical union with the female, man would become complete and achieve gnosis."

Harmston's use of Shekinah and the information on the websites is too close to be coincidence. Although Harmston is not known to use Shekinah in reference to ritual sex in his endowment house, there have been references in other groups. It is well known that John Bryant, who splintered from AUB with a small following in the 1970s, practiced ritual sex as part of the temple endowment.[19]

Doug recovered and wanted to sell out and move to Manti, but Kaziah refused. The Indianola ranch was the fulfillment of a lifelong dream. Doug once again became sullen and withdrew his affection. In the meantime Doug had taken two more wives, LePrele and Rose. Rose, like one of Harmston's eight wives, Anna Mae, was a widow of Ervil LeBaron. After much mental anguish, Kaziah finally agreed to sell.

Harmston ignored Doug's version of consecration and instituted his own. The procedure dictated that the wife was to consecrate to the husband, who then consecrated to James D. Harmston. Kaziah said that Harmston had Doug wrapped around his little finger. "If I consecrated to Doug, Harmston knew the money was just as good his."

To help induce Kaziah's cooperation, women's classes teaching the true order of consecration were conducted, Kaziah believes, for her benefit. In addition Harmston gave Kaziah a blessing in which he revealed that in a previous life[20] she had been one of Jesus Christ's plural wives. He also promised her that if she submitted to a full consecration she would never want for anything the rest of her life. Full consecration meant she would legally turn over everything she owned to Doug, who would legally turn it over to Harmston.

Harmston also introduced his version of the Church of the Firstborn, which constituted a step higher than belonging to the TLC. In the Church of the Firstborn a member received his Second Anointing and his Calling & Election Made Sure (temple ordinances practiced by the early LDS Church). The First Anointing is the Temple Endowment, where commitments are made to God. The Second Anointing is where your exaltation is made sure, you can no longer sin, and according to Harmston, you may meet Christ face to face.

The Church of the Firstborn was the prestigious place where loyal TLC members sought to be, where members received a "white apron." Harmston's white apron was hemmed with gold thread designating him as being the prophet with the most priesthood. However, a full and complete consecration was a prerequisite to membership in the Church of the Firstborn.

At a meeting with the TLC bishopric, Kaziah said she was promised that she would receive a stewardship of property within the Shekinah where she could raise her precious goats. Doug, as an apostle and the man over consecration, made the same promise. Harmston had also promised that at a special meeting of the members of the Church of the Firstborn, she would see Jesus Christ face to face.

They sold the property in three separate parcels. As head of the family, Doug took custody of the money and began consecrating cash directly into Harmston's hands. He dished out cash, wrote checks, and threw fancy dinners for the apostles like he was the king of the hill. While the money lasted, Doug was the big man in the TLC, supporting all the apostles who were advised by Harmston not to work, but devote their energies to the building of the kingdom of God.

It hurt Kaziah that LePrele and Rose, who came in the family dead broke, received their white aprons first. And of course, when the coveted time came for Kaziah and others to meet Christ face to face, he didn't show, except in the spirit which only two people were spiritually strong enough to witness, Harmston and his daughter.

They used some of the money to purchase an older home in Manti that Kaziah single handedly remodeled. Kaziah didn't receive her stewardship of land, and when Doug had spent all their money, Kaziah was forced to go to the bishop and ask for money to pay utility bills. The bishop, Bill Lithgow, consulted Harmston, who told him "no." He was getting ready to excommunicate Doug and he knew Kaziah would follow Doug. It would be tantamount to wasted money.

Doug, who had made the down payment on the church's meeting hall, got on the wrong side of Harmston when he challenged his authority. In a blessing given by church patriarch Phil Savage, Doug had been told that in a previous life he had been a brother of Adam, and Adam was the god of this world. In Doug's mind that put him on an even footing with Harmston, who was supposed to be the reincarnated Joseph Smith. While working on a painting for the meeting house, it dawned on Doug that Harmston was getting ready to declare himself Jesus Christ. Doug confronted Harmston and told him that no way he was Jesus Christ.

True to form, Kaziah followed Doug after his excommunication. Doug then divorced Kaziah, abandoned Rose, and married LePrele. Doug and LePrele had Doug's pension to live on. Kaziah had nothing but the house. Completely devastated, Kaziah contemplated suicide as a way out when she and Cindy Stewart teamed up. Kaziah said she felt like she had been spiritually raped. The lawsuit was their way of fighting back and regaining their self respect.

Harmston had talked Cindy into cashing in her 401 (k) worth $12,000. He promised to pay her back, but when she asked for the money, he told she had consecrated the money. He then excommunicated her.

At first, Doug was amiable and cooperated as a co-plaintiff in the lawsuit. But after a clandestine visit from Harmston, Doug withdrew as a co-plaintiff and he and LePrele turned completely against Kaziah. Doug changed his testimony and claimed Kaziah had consecrated the money with no strings attached. During the trial in 2001, Doug was humiliated and impeached when I played my tape recorded interview with Doug for the jury, and the truth was revealed.

A jury awarded Kaziah $500,000 and Cindy $50,000. However, that was not the end. Harmston's attorneys found procedural questions of law and persuaded the Judge to overrule the jury verdict and grant them a new trial. However, Kaziah opted to appeal to the Utah Supreme Court where the case will sit for at least two years.

Tom Green was paralegal in the Kaziah Hancock vs. Harmston lawsuit. Tom wanted to meet Kaziah so he and Bill Aldrich rode with me to serve papers on Harmston and other defendants in the TLC hierarchy. Harmston knew Tom and told him it was despicable for one polygamist to work against another. Tom replied he was just doing his job as paralegal. But reflecting back, I think Tom had something else in mind. I think Tom wanted to look over Kaziah to see if he might like to recruit her into his polygamist family. As it turned out, Kaziah became friendly with Tapestry Against Polygamy and, under their influence, developed an intense dislike for Tom.

After the Hancock lawsuit was filed in 1998, *The Salt Lake Tribune* reporter Dan Egan wrote a story that was published April 10, 1998. A few days after the story, a sinister looking man with dark hair and beard walked into the Tribune Building, confronted a secretary, and said that while eating breakfast at the Village Inn he overheard two men in the next booth plotting to assassinate Dan Egan. He thought the two men were Harmston's henchmen and left before the secretary could get his name.

Dan Egan called me and asked what I thought. I knew immediately the identity of the sinister man. The Village Inn is John C. Putvin's favorite place to eat. I assured Dan it was a hoax because it didn't fit the profile of Harmston and was a stunt Putvin would pull. A few days later, in a telephone call to Rod Williams, Putvin admitted that it was him.

James D. Harmston is one of the most ruthless and cold-hearted polygamist leaders in the subculture. According to Kaziah, in 1994 Harmston sent his apostles to Washington D.C to place a curse on the White House. He also sent them to curse all the Mormon temples except the Manti Temple, which he expects to take over. Harmston had taught that he will one day walk down South Temple Street in Salt Lake City and "zap" all the church buildings and apostles. He has promised old women that if they will sell their homes and consecrate the money to him he can guarantee their exaltation in the celestial kingdom. Before Kaziah left the TLC, a college professor sold his home and turned $120,000 over to Harmston. Two weeks later he was excommunicated. I talked with the college professor who said it was quite a learning experience.

In 1998 Harmston is alleged to have taken a sixteen-year-old girl as a plural wife and impregnated her. To cover up his crime he arranged for her to legally marry a boy near her own age. Rodney Clowdus, a disenchanted TLC member, concealed a tape recorder in his shirt and inveigled Harmston into a conversation in which Harmston admitted to the marriage. Harmston claimed he was commanded by an angel to marry the girl, which he did, reluctantly. She was a gift, he explained, and was to be the mother of a special child. Harmston then preceded to tell Clowdus that "Angie" was an inexperienced lover but a great cuddler. A copy of the tape recording was given to the author and a member of the press. The original tape recording was turned over to the San Pete County Sheriff's Office, and there the matter died.

Like Owen Allred and AUB, Harmston and the TLC have attempted to supplant the LDS Church. Both AUB and TLC claim they are the only religious organization on earth that is living all of God's laws. Swindling Cindy Stewart out of her 401 (k) and taking sexual advantage of a sixteen-year-old girl is a justifiable part of Harmston's religion, he believes.

The question to be asked is, how culpable is religion in the committing of Harmston's alleged crimes? Does the religion encourage the committing of crime, or does the criminal wrongly use religion to commit a crime? When the same religion, Mormon Fundamentalism, is used by four different polygamist groups to commit crime, what does that say about the religion?

James D. Harmston is one of the most innovative of the polygamist prophets. His first wife Elaine is a necromancer. She has a special, pink room with an alter where she communicates with the dead ancestors of TLC members to see if the dead would like to be proxy-baptized into the TLC. Rodney Clowdus gave the author a copy of a transcript where Elaine communicated with one of Clowdus' dead ancestors.

Multiple Mortal Probation, as I've explained before, has been one of Harmston's strongest convert inducements, a major self esteem builder. A man of simple status in this life can learn that he was a *great man* in a previous life. Harmston would explain that in previous lives, he was Isaiah, King Arthur, Joseph Smith, and after he saw the movie *Braveheart* suddenly remembered he was also William Wallace.

Chapter Six

Tom Green and His Wives

When Tom Green was appearing on all the TV shows, he lived in Snake Valley near the Granite Ranch, and called his place Greenhaven. Like Pleasant Valley, it was a cluster of about sixteen old house trailers that Tom and Bill Aldrich had dragged 100 miles across the sagebrush desert.

Pleasant Valley, the home of Dennis Matthews, was about sixteen miles due west just inside the Nevada border. All the kids in Snake Valley, including the kids from Pleasant Valley, were bused to the West Deseret School that was about three miles from Greenhaven. At Boy Scout meetings the Matthews' kids interacted with the Green kids.

Tom and Dennis Matthews were converted to Mormon Fundamentalism about the same time and had attended the same underground, cottage proselyting sessions. Tom said that he and Dennis discussed what polygamous group they should attempt to join. Tom chose the Peterson Group (The Righteous Branch), a small offshoot of the Allred Group (AUB). According to Tom, Matthews chose the Allred Group because that's where most of the available girls could be found. Tom became an apostle in the Peterson Group, and Matthews married a daughter of Ormand Lavery, one of Owen's apostles.

Back in 1997, Tom had his family living in an apartment in West Jordan, Utah. Just as Tom had been the paralegal in the Kaziah Hancock vs. Harmston lawsuit, so too was he the paralegal in the

Virginia Hill case. On two occasions I met Tom at the apartment either picking up or dropping off documents for Don Redd. The apartment was crawling with young girls and kids.

Tom then moved his family to a larger, nicer apartment in Sandy, Utah, just off Fort Union Blvd. One day I dropped off some tape recordings for Tom and was met at the door by a cute blonde girl who looked no older than sixteen. I assumed she was a younger sister of one of his wives, or possibly Tom's daughter. It did not occur to me that she was Tom's youngest wife, Hannah.

Later, when I found out the blonde girl was Tom's wife with one child, I was shocked. I couldn't imagine why a pretty young girl would want to marry Tom in his late forties. Nor could I understand how a father or mother would allow their daughter to marry Tom. I was tempted to say something to Tom but didn't. Tom seemed to be doing an excellent job as a paralegal and I didn't want to cause a problem that might jeopardize the case. I got to know Tom very well as we worked together on the Hill case.

News of the criminal prosecution of Tom Green spread across the United States and around the world. He was scrutinized by all the major news stations and appeared as a guest on all the major talk shows. Media from France, Germany, Canada, Japan, and the United Kingdom came to Utah to interview Tom and his wives. Helicopters transported reporters and camera men back and forth between Greenhaven in the west desert and Salt Lake City. I watched as Tom's media image became the most important thing in his life.

Everything came to a stop when the media came to call. His paralegal work in the Virginia Hill case and even his own criminal defense took a backseat to media interviews. He was flamboyant, unafraid, and articulate, but because he was an audacious nonconformist, he was held in contempt by his fellow polygamists. Whatever Tom was, he would have been a nobody without his five little wives.

Tom has a number of good qualities. He's bright, well read,

congenial, and has an excellent memory for detail. But by any standard, he is not a handsome man. What then was there about Tom that attracted these young wives, who seem very devoted to Tom? Why would a pretty fourteen-year-old girl like his youngest wife Hannah, want to marry a man in his forties? Why would they choose to live in near squalor conditions that is little more than camping out on the desert?

Each of Tom's young wives are the products of one hundred years of Fundamentalist indoctrination. Polygamy, public welfare lines, and secretive religion is how they have been raised. Their world is as alien to mainstream Americans as would be Iran's Islam life.

Wife Beth Cook

Tom's first wife was Lynda Penman, now deceased. They married in 1970 and divorced in 1984. Prior to the divorce, Tom married Beth Cook in a spiritual wedding. Tom had met Beth at a cottage meeting.

When Beth was twelve years old, Roy Johnson, the leader at Short Creek, gave Beth as a plural wife to a man old enough to be her grandpa. He also gave Beth's nine-year-old sister to the same man. Beth freed herself from the oppressive FLDS, but she is still tied to the doctrines of Mormon Fundamentalism and she implanted those doctrines into the psyche of her daughters.

Next Tom spiritually married Beth's young daughter Linda Kunz. Then Beth introduced Tom to her half sister June Johnson and to June's daughters, the Beagley girls, who were all living in Colorado City. Beth left Tom in 1989, when Tom placed young Linda over her mother Beth as head wife.

As you will discover, Tom liked his new wives young, which is evident by their tender ages: 12, 13, 14 and 15. According to Jeremy Aldrich, the son of Bill Aldrich, Tom advised Jeremy to marry his wives young so he could train them the way he wanted them.

Wife Linda Kunz

Tom *legally married* fourteen-year-old Linda on December 19, 1986. Linda's first child, Melvin, was born October 16, 1986. Counting backwards, Juab County Attorney David Leavitt determined that Melvin was full term, making Linda thirteen when she conceived. In April 2000 Leavitt charged Tom with four counts of Bigamy, one count of Criminal Non Support, and Child Rape. In essence, he threw the book at Tom.

Where Linda conceived became an issue during the trial. I was still friends with Tom in 2000 and Tom assured me that Linda was fourteen when she conceived, which satisfied the law at that time. He was cock-sure that the Child Rape charge would be the easiest to beat. He said that Linda conceived in Wyoming, not Utah.

When David Leavitt revealed that Linda was thirteen when she conceived, Tom changed his story and told me that she had actually conceived in Mexico. He said that Linda was anxious to get married, but his sister threatened to report them if they married in Utah, so they went to Mexico. I said to Tom, "You told me Linda conceived in Wyoming." He explained that he had forgotten and that Linda had reminded him they went to Mexico directly from Wyoming where they got married and she conceived.

I later interviewed Stan Shepp, an adopted son of Tom Green. Stan said that he was told by Tom that Linda conceived in Idaho. But Linda testified in court that she conceived in Mexico, and as proof, Attorney John Bucher imported a polygamist from Mexico who testified that he attended the wedding. However, when it was discovered by the prosecution that if a crime is planned in Utah but the defendant goes outside the state to commit the crime to avoid prosecution, Utah has joint jurisdiction. On that basis Tom was convicted of child rape.

Linda has six children by Tom.

Wife June Johnson

June Johnson, half sister to Beth Cook and the mother of Shirley and LeeAnn Beagley, became Tom's plural wife in 1987.

She had four children by Tom. June later separated from Tom for the same reasons as Beth, but continued to live at Greenhaven in a separate trailer so her children would be close to their father.

Wife Shirley Beagley

In 1986 sixteen-year-old Shirley Beagley knew that she was about to placed by the FLDS priesthood into a family as a plural wife. At sixteen she chose to marry Tom rather than wait to be placed with someone not of her choosing. They subsequently had six children.

Wife Allison Ryan

Allison Ryan married Tom at age sixteen. It was a spiritual wedding. Allison was a neighbor girl with problems at home, who was befriended by Linda and Shirley. She was not raised in the polygamist subculture. In 1990 Allison tired of Tom and the stresses of plural life and fled to Idaho. There were no children. Allison testified against Tom at his bigamy trial.

Wife LeeAnn Beagley

LeeAnn Beagley, the daughter of June Johnson and sister of Shirley Beagley, was legally married to Tom at age fourteen. When LeeAnn was a student in Middle School, she told her counselor that she was being pressured into marrying an old man. Tom had LeeAnn shipped down to live with Bill Aldrich at the Cane Beds in Southern Utah. When LeeAnn told Bill that Tom had molested her, Bill took LeeAnn to her aunt in Colorado City. The aunt reported the matter to the juvenile authorities in St. George, Utah.

There was an investigation. But after her mother June and Beth Cook, who are half sisters, had a good talk with LeeAnn, she changed her story and said she was not molested. Shortly thereafter, LeeAnn married Tom. She has five children by Tom.

LeeAnn's change of story became an issue in the bigamy trial but LeeAnn stuck to her last story. After Tom was convicted of Child Rape, and with the help of prosecutor David Leavitt, LeeAnn left Tom. According to a confidential informant, after LeeAnn left Tom she admitted that everything bad that was said about Tom was true.

Wives Cari & Hannah Bjorkman

Cari Bjorkman, age fifteen, became Tom's plural wife in 1991. She has three children by Tom.

Hannah Leigh Bjorkman, age fourteen, legally married forty-one year old Tom in September 27, 1991. Cari and Hannah are the daughters of fundamentalist parents living in Snake Valley near Greenhaven. According to Bill Aldrich, Tom talked the mother of the girls into letting him take them to New York City to babysit the Green children while Tom and his wives were guests on a television talk show. Bill said that Tom confided in him that the two Bjorkman girls and his wives had a sexual party in the New York hotel. When the Bjorkman girls arrived home they couldn't wait to become plural wives, but Karen, the girls' mother, wouldn't let Hannah marry until she turned fourteen.

Karen, the mother of the Bjorkman girls, became the plural wife of Tom's adopted son Steve McKinley. The marriage only lasted a couple of years. The father of the girls was a bee keeper and seldom home.

Tom married and divorced his wives one by one believing he was circumventing the bigamy laws. Tom legally married his fourteen-year-old wives so he couldn't be charged with sex with a minor.

On March 19, 1996, Tom and Julie Dawn McKinley, age fifteen, applied for a marriage license in Salt Lake City. Julie was the daughter of Tom's adopted son Steven B. McKinley. Steve authorized the marriage and even tried to perform the marriage ceremony in the hallway. But a Juvenile Court Judge rescinded permission for Julie to marry. Shortly thereafter, Julie lost interest in Tom and Fundamentalism. Julie Dawn was able to avoid contact with the media and state investigators during Tom's trial.

An essential element of Utah's bigamy statue states that a man commits bigamy when he marries a second wife while still married to the legal wife. Tom was not legally married when he was charged with bigamy and thought he was home free, when the unexpected happened. The court ruled that under Utah Code 30-4.5, a man and woman living together as husband and wife, rearing children together, in spite of a previous divorce, are common law spouses. The court chose Linda, the head wife, and made her Tom's legal wife.

This is a good time to explain the significance of adopted sons. One of the mysteries of early Mormonism is the Law of Adoption. The early church leaders had men ceremoniously sealed to them much the same way as women were sealed. The idea was to form one great family united by a religious ordinance. Apostles like Brigham Young were sealed to Joseph Smith. One of Brigham's adopted sons was the infamous John D. Lee, the Mountain Meadows Massacre scapegoat. Early loyal Mormons seemed to think that if they were sealed to a Mormon icon like Brigham Young, it would enhance their chances of making it to the celestial kingdom.

Tom Green maintained that his priesthood did not involve organizing polygamist groups, but family. One day while working on the Virginia Hill lawsuit, he told me that he would be away in the mountains for the next two weeks at a family reunion. It wasn't until later that I learned that by family reunion, he meant a meeting with his adopted sons and their posterity. The reunion was much more than a social gathering, it was a miniature "general conference."

Tom claims to be the only one holding the patriarchal keys in the Church of the Firstborn. He was the head of a family organization that consisted at the time of about five adopted sons and their families. The government of this family consisted of a council over which Tom presided. Tom traveled among independent fundamentalists proselyting his particular brand of Mormonism. In other words, Tom was looking for more young wives and more adopted sons. When Tom came to visit, it was the habit of one fundamentalist mother to place rings on the wedding fingers of her single daughters.

When I first met Tom I made it clear that I no longer believed in Mormon Fundamentalism and did not want anything to do with any organized religion. Consequently, he did not try to proselyte me. However, Tom did attempt to entice Rod Williams, until Rod shut him down.

Tom was patriarch, savior, father, husband, and lover to his wives, all wrapped into one. All the girls came from extremely humble circumstances. Tom united them into a common family. He took them from the dower sage flats of Utah's west desert to the bright lights of New York City. They flew in airplanes, dined and slept in the best hotels, and were treated like celebrities.

Tom had convinced them that they were the instruments that God would use to show the world that polygamy was a workable alternative form of marriage and that all the polygamists in Utah and Arizona would be eternally in their debt. They were having fun in taking the lead in a great cause. It was a grand adventure while it lasted.

The Green wives believe in the same Mormon principles as their polygamist neighbors and orthodox Latter-day Saints. But when it comes to Tom's authority, the rest of Mormondom believe the girls have been deceived or they are deluded. Nevertheless, as wives and mothers they are to be admired because they have demonstrated a cohesive quality and determination equivalent to their pioneer ancestors.

A tragic event occurred to them in 1997. Tom and his family had been evicted from a Sandy, Utah, trailer court and moved to Snake Valley on a ten acre sagebrush plot with an old cabin. The nearest pavement was 100 miles away. The nearest neighbor was the Anderson ranch a mile away.

On January 14, 1997, except for Linda, Cari, and the children, Tom and the rest of the wives were away on one of Tom's many proselyting excursions. At 2:00 a.m. the smoke alarm sounded in the laundry. Linda leaped out of bed and ran to the laundry room where a pile of dirty clothes was engulfed in flames. She ran to where Cari was sleeping and yelled, "The house is on fire, get the kids out!"

While Cari herded the children towards the front door, Linda grabbed an old fire extinguisher, but in her panic could not get it to work. By then the flames had spread from the laundry room and the house was filling with dark smoke.

It was pitch black outside. The temperature was ten degrees below zero with eight inches of snow on the ground. There was no time to salvage clothes, all they had on was their pajamas. Fortunately, Linda had pulled on a pair of wool socks before she went to bed.

As they huddled together, Cari made a head-count of the children. To her horror, three year-old Jerry was missing. Without hesitating, Linda took a deep breath and rushed back into the cabin. She was blinded by the billowing smoke. Her eyes burning, she probed until she found Jerry's bed and felt his little body. At her touch he started to sob. And then she heard another child crying somewhere in the smoke filled room.

She set Jerry on the floor and gently pushed him in the direction of the door. Her eyes blurred by smoke and tears, she stumbled towards the sound of the crying child. She snatched him up and headed for the door. Now she was choking and coughing. As she passed through the bedroom door she grabbed what she thought was Jerry's uplifted hand. But when she finally made it outside, it was a little girl, not Jerry.

She turned to go back inside but by then the flames had closed in behind her. The cabin was a burning inferno. She ran behind the house and broke out the bedroom window. It was her intention to climb through the window and try and find Jerry, but the superheated smoke drove her back. There was nothing more she could do to save little Jerry.

Mrs. Anderson, a mile away, got up to use the bathroom and saw the flames from her window. She quickly telephoned other nearby ranchers and she and her husband drove as fast as they could to the Green cabin.

It was thirty minutes before the Andersons arrived. By then the cabin was totally gutted with just a few flames left to give a little light. Not a soul was in sight. At first Mrs. Anderson was afraid that the Greens had all perished in the fire until she saw footprints in the snow leading to an old trailer forty yards away. Inside the trailer Linda, Cari, and more than a dozen children huddled under a tattered sleeping bag.

The ranchers in Snake Valley and the LDS Church Relief Society (women's organization) in the town of Delta rallied to assist the Green family. A rancher in the settlement of Caliao, once a stagecoach and Pony Express Station, let the Greens use an old vacant ranch house until Tom could reestablish the family in house trailers.

Juab County prosecutor David Leavitt suggested that Tom's wives were victims of the "Stockholm Syndrome." For those unfamiliar with the Stockholm Syndrome, it is a situation where female victims held hostage fall in love with or become emotionally connected to their captors. Patty Hearst, granddaughter of newspaper publisher William Randolph Hearst, was kidnaped by a terrorist group calling themselves the Symbionese Liberation Army (SLA). Before Patty was rescued she participated in a bank robbery. She has since been de-programed and rehabilitated.

Another theory that could explain the attraction of these young girls to Tom Green is Sigmund Freud's "Oedipus Complex." Freud proposed that people were often subject to an early "phallic" state of development where children were erotically attached to a parent of the opposite sex, and hostile to the parent of the same sex.

This theory would appear to be applicable in Linda's case. According to witnesses, Linda became erotically involved with Tom at age twelve. When Linda was fourteen, Tom made her titular head of the family over her own mother. Linda did not seem to have a problem with presiding over her mother.

As a law enforcement sex crime investigator, I saw this same phenomena in other molest cases, especially where the victim was a willing participant like Linda. Under such circumstances, it was not unusual for the daughter to challenge the mother for female dominance in the home.

The way a woman (polygamist or not) feels, believes, and acts is very much connected to how she was raised. Women are not treated the same throughout the fundamentalist subculture. Generally speaking, among most independents and in the Allred Group (AUB), the women have as much freedom as monogamous women. The adhesiveness that binds them to the family or group can be a combination of several things, not all necessarily religious.

Unlike in the FLDS, a woman is entitled to pick the family where she will become a plural wife, and she can go into the family without any assets to speak of. If the man can afford to receive her, he is obligated. Security is therefore one reason women chose polygamy.

If the woman is attractive or wealthy, a man may ask the prophet permission to court her. Competing for an eligible woman can be quite humorous. An interested man may send one of his wives to make friends with the woman and induce her. Or, he might manufacture excuses to be near her where he will strut and plume like a peacock. Sometimes a father will guide one of his daughters into a particular family to create family ties. In the 1950s and 1960s the AUB apostles had managed to trade daughters as wives until the Jessop, Allred, Jenson, Lavery, and Thompson families were all interrelated. The most acceptable and common method for obtaining a plural wife is when the women recruit other women.

In the Allred Group (AUB) it is a safe estimate that less than half of the men and women who convert to their group last longer than five years. People come and go like a revolving door. It is the girls and boys who are born and reared in the subculture who are more apt to stay. In those cases, the kids are as converted to the society as they are to the religion. Even then, at least 65 percent or more of the kids choose to leave the subculture, especially if they were reared by a second rate wife.

No matter how hard a husband tries, he will not be completely fair. There is no such thing as equality in plural marriage. Some men don't even try; they have their favorites where they spend the majority of their time. Some men place their second rate wives in trailers located at inexpensive locations like Pleasant Valley or the Granite Ranch.

Some plural wives, like Kathleen Covington who was a plural wife to Dennis Matthews, are inculcated with the doctrine that only a husband can resurrect a women, during what many religious faiths call the Resurrection. She said that no matter how many times she went to Owen Allred and complained about Dennis' neglect, she was told to be a good wife and perceiver.

First Rate or Second Rate

In all of the polygamist groups, there are the "blue blood" families, the elite who get special privileges. The kids in the elite families are cliquish and find subtle ways to squelch the kids in second-rate families. In each group, there are the favorite wives and their children, and then those who are not the favorites. And some men are considered more powerful and others less so. Thus terms like first-rate and second-rate are understood by the members.

The exhilaration and adventure of secrecy are highly contributing reasons for people, men especially, to convert to polygamy. It is a favorite pastime for converts to get together and exchange close-call stories of how they were nearly caught, as they try to hide it from friends, relatives, and employers.

Two views of the road in Utah's west desert that leads to Greenhaven, Tom Green's former family compound in the Snake Valley.

Tom Green's former family compound in the Snake Valley.

An ariel view of Tom Green's former family compound in the Snake Valley.

An ariel view of Tom Green's former family compound in the Snake Valley.

Green family, 1999.

Center: Tom Green.
Tom Green's wives, clockwise from top: Linda Kunz, Hannah Bjorkman,
LeeAnn Beagley, Shirley Beagley, Cari Bjorkman

Tom Green with wives, Hannah Bjorkman and Shirley Beagley, with a few of their children outside the courtroom in Juab County.

Tom Green and Bill Aldrich.

Steve McKenley

Lt. Ron Barton
Investigator for the A.G. office in Utah.

Utah Attorney General,
Mark Shurtleff.

Juab County Attorney, David Leavitt.

Ben Bistline, Historian

Independent polygamist, Steve Butt.

Independent polygamist, Ogden Kraut and his wife Ann Wilde.

TLC Prophet James D. Harmston in Manti, Utah.

Kaziah May Hancock

Tapestry Against Polygamy Co-founder, Vicky Prunty.

Tapestry Against Polygamy Co-founder, Rowenna Erickson.

Organizer of Help The Child Brides, Bob Curran.

AUB's Council and Apostles, 1990.
Standing, left to right: Orman Lavery (deceased), Owen A. Allred, Marvin
Allred (deceased), Joseph Thompson (deceased), Bill Baird (deceased).
Sitting, left to right: Lynn Thompson, George Maycock (excommunicated),
J. LaMoine Jenson, Marvin Jessop, Morris Jessop.

Left to right: Investigator, Rod Williams,
John Shugart and Attorney Don Redd.

AUB's Prophet,
Owen A. Allred.

Dennis Matthews

David O. Kingston

Prophet Paul Kingston

John D. Kingston

*Mary Ann Kingston, daughter of John D. Kingston
who forced her to marry her uncle, David O. Kingston.*

*Left to right: Rulon Jeffs, current FLDS Prophet Warren Jeffs,
and Colorado City Mayor, Dan Barlow.*

Winston Blackmore

Ruby Jessop

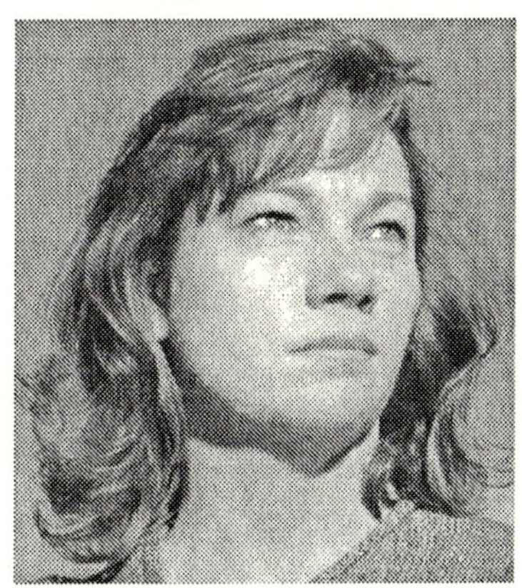

Laura Chapman

Arizona Attorney General,
Terry Goddard.

Polygamist home in Rocky Ridge, ???

Don Lafferty at the Utah State Prison.

Brian David Mitchell, self proclaimed prophet Immanuel.

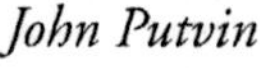

John Putvin

Chapter Seven

Bleeding the Beast for Your Tax Dollars

There is a euphemism coined by contemporary polygamists labeling those polygamists who choose to deliberately plunder state and federal welfare. It is called "bleeding the beast." Bleeding the beast is practiced in all the polygamist groups at varying frequency.

There is no sin in bleeding the beast because the "beast" deserves it, they claim. But who is the "beast" really? It is you, and the hard earned tax dollars you pay to the government. So who makes it possible for these polygamists to survive, who supports them financially? It is you and me.

The following sermon by James D. Harmston epitomizes the general thinking of those Mormon Fundamentalists who exploit the welfare system. The sermon is a paraphrased but accurate version submitted by Kaziah May Hancock and Cindy Stewart who state they have heard Harmston preach the sermon more than once.

You people need to swallow your pride and take advantage of every government assistance program there is. That's what God wants. He doesn't expect you to wallow in turkey manure. In another lifetime, we were persecuted and thrown out of Jackson County by the government. We're entitled to everything we can get.

Tom Green is a classic example of bleeding the beast. Tom was a master welfare recipient, a professional bleeder who harvested by the bucket. According to Bill Aldrich, he sat down at the kitchen table and with paper and pencil, figured out how much each wife could bring in; then he instructed his wives to enroll in every state and federal welfare program where by hook or crook they could qualify.

Tom claimed to be a professional magazine salesman but Bill Aldrich said that in the three years he lived with Tom, he only worked as selling magazines for one month, and then his wives did most of the work while he supervised.

In August 2001, Tom was convicted of Bigamy and Criminal Non Support. According to Utah Attorney General Investigators Lt. Ron Barton and Diana Hollis, Tom's income from selling magazines was as follows: $23,400 in 1995; $16,000 in 1996; $3,950 in 1997; and $2,850 in 1998.

Tom claimed that his declining income from magazine sales was due to an eviction from a Sandy trailer park, his move to Greenhaven, and the fire in which his three year-old son died.

It is interesting to note that from 1998 to 1999, even though he was active in granting television interviews and receiving payments for that, Tom bled the beast by the bucketfuls.

Your tax dollars were hard at work. Investigators Barton and Hollis documented a total of $647,263.45 during the years 1998 and 1999. That figure only represents those amounts where documentation was still available. Barton and Hollis estimated that if they had been able to access a complete documentation of all the state and federal programs where the Green family is known to have received assistance, going back to when Tom married his first plural wife, the figure would be well over $1,000,000, possibly as much as $1,500,000. The breakdown for the years 1998 and 1999 are as follows:

Food stamps	$203,874
Financial aid	130,255
Medical & dental	74,350
Pharmaceutical	7,195
Hospitalization	213,268
Child care	13,528
WIC	4,791

The hospital expenses were due to a birth defect in one of his daughters. When they enrolled the child at Primary Children's Hospital, Tom, who has always been proud that he fathered many children, acknowledged on the admitting form that he was the father. Tom said that had they claimed the father was unknown, he wouldn't have been obligated to pay.

In 1997, Tom met with Recovery Services and was given the opportunity to pay back $78,000 in monthly payments, a figure substantially less than the $213,268.49. Tom agreed, but after repeated reminders, six to be exact, Tom never paid a penny. And even if he was sincere about paying back the money, he wasn't working.

Tom set up a trust he named "Order of Saint Michael." Aldrich said Tom wanted the trust to sound Catholic to throw suspicion off his polygamist activities. All of the Greenhaven assets were protected by the trust. Aldrich said that Tom used his name as a front trustee of the trust.

The Order of Saint Michael ostensibly rented a trailer to each wife for $400 per month. The State of Utah (and its taxpaying citizens) helped the girls make the monthly payments. Then Saint Michael set up an exclusive day care center for his children, managed by their mothers. The State (and its taxpaying citizens) helped out again.

Tom never passed up a chance to save a dollar or make an easy buck. Although his kids were home taught, he sent them to the West Desert Public School for free breakfast and lunch.

I asked Tom why he consented to appear on television shows where he knew he was going to be humiliated like on the Judge Judy Show. While Tom and two of his wives stood before Judge Judy, she demanded to know about his welfare scams. Tom's justification has always been that if it is there and his wives qualify, then they are entitled to it. Judy accused him of bilking the taxpayers and ordered him off the set.

Tom's reply to my question was that he and his family were on a divine mission to demonstrate to the world the virtues of polygamy. Two weeks before he went to prison I asked him again. This time he said Judge Judy paid for his entire family to visit Disneyland.

Investigators Barton and Hollis obtained receipts showing that Tom received $1200 over and above expenses for appearing on the Sally show. He received $1450 for appearing on the Queen Latifah Show. Beth Cook, the mother of Linda, received enough from an interview to purchase Tom's kids a trampoline set and still have $1000 left over.

Before Tom went to prison he confided that he had selected Carolyn Campbell, a local writer, to write his biography. He thought publishers would be stumbling over each other to sign him up. He figured that between advances, royalties, and movie rights, he would make a million dollars. He said that while he was in prison he was going to send his wives around the country on a speaking tour. He said that at the moment, Linda and one other wife were in Seattle doing a show in which they would be paid $1000 over expenses. He predicted that by the time he got out of prison he would be a wealthy man. He also said that all of the proceeds from the book, movies, and speaking tour would go into The Order of Saint Michael.

Carolyn had contacted an interested literary agent who was uneasy with The Order of Saint Michael and how Tom was manipulating things. The agent asked Carolyn if Utah had a "Son of Sam" law that prevents a convicted felon from profiting from his crime. (There is no Son of Sam law in Utah[21].) The agent also said that the book must include the prosecution side of the story as well as Tom's side, which presented the following problem.

The prosecution had subpoenaed Carolyn concerning a magazine story she had written about Tom and his family a few years previous. She did not want to testify so she obtained an attorney, claiming that as a journalist her testimony was privileged. Her refusal to testify put her on a bad footing with prosecutor David Leavitt, which she felt would hamper Leavitt's cooperation in writing the prosecution side of the story.

Therefore, she asked me if I would do the prosecution side of the story.

I agreed providing I had absolute freedom to do it. I knew Tom well enough to know he would want me to slant my writing to make Leavitt look bad. To make sure Tom understood, I arranged to visit him in prison where I told him I could not be involved in a whitewash. I also told him that if I discovered that he had committed any other crimes, I would not cover it up. He said he had no problems with my position and knew of no other crimes that he could be accused of.

I contacted Investigator Ron Barton who had no problems with my doing the prosecution side of the story. We exchanged information and he gave me the names, addresses, and phone numbers of all the prosecution witnesses. He also said I was perfectly free to contact any of the witnesses.

I first contacted what I perceived as the prosecution's key witnesses. At that time, the child rape charge was still pending. For me the child rape charge was the most intriguing because it was the most serious.

Within a week I received a phone call from Tom's attorney John Bucher, who was upset that I was talking to witnesses. He said I wasn't supposed to be writing about the child rape and wanted me to stop. Of course I refused. I wasn't telling him how to lawyer and I resented him telling me what I could write. He said he would instruct all of his witnesses not to talk to me. The next day, Beth Cook started an email campaign accusing me of being in David Leavitt's employ. I was no longer welcome as a co-author.

I continued to attend all the court hearings leading up to the child rape trial. One day David Leavitt pulled me aside and asked if he were to subpoena me, would I claim reporter privilege. I told him no, I would tell the truth.

At the next hearing I testified that Tom had told me he went to Mexico to marry Linda because his sister threatened to report him to the police for marrying a thirteen-year-old girl.

Now back to bleeding the beast. State and federal welfare programs (and you taxpaying citizens) paid for coal and butane to heat the Green's trailers. Taxpayers paid for food, child care, hospitalization, medication, and therapy for two of Tom's children who had physical defects. Government did everything for the Green family except cook the food, wash the dishes, and do the laundry. And according to Investigator Barton, there were other perks Tom's family received that you can't attach a dollar sign to, like Sub for Santa and food banks. It became apparent for everyone to see that Tom's philosophy was the more wives and children the more dollars in his pocket.

There seems to be little shame among some polygamists when it comes to profiting from welfare. Flora Jessop, a dissident from Colorado City, said that when some women in the FLDS become pregnant they pray for a Downs Syndrome child so they can get more welfare assistance.

In 1998, Tom Zoellner, reporter for *The Salt Lake Tribune,* conducted an in-depth investigation into the welfare practices of the FLDS. The completed story which appeared June 28th shocked Utah taxpayers.

The combined population of Colorado City and Hildale at the time was estimated at 5,274.[22] One third of that number accepted food stamps to help support their large families.

Colorado City and Hildale are among the top ten towns in the Intermountain West that receive help from the WIC (Women, Infants and Children) program. Their ratio for using U.S. Department of Agriculture food stamps is 33 percent as compared to the rest of Arizona, 6.7 percent, and Utah 4.7 percent.

Zoellner reported "Hildale was awarded $405,006.00 in federal housing grants to refurbish 19 homes on church-owned land. And that Mayor David Zitting, a member of the FLDS Church, was appointed by two Utah governors (Republicans Norm Bangerter and Mike Leavitt) to sit on the state Housing Development Advisory Council." Hildale ranks last in average taxes paid ($651 annually), and No. 1 in exemptions (3.62).

Zoellner presented figures on average household income and per capita income that in both towns seriously questioned whether residents could feed or clothe their children without taxpayer assistance.

In 1998, Colorado City and Hildale had a combined budget of $13 million dollars to support two colleges, a small industrial park, a school district, a power plant, a radio station, and two city governments.

Zoellner reported that FLDS resident Joe Knudson contended that most of the government sponsored programs went to feed and raise great honest kids. He said, "Dollars and cents later, you're ending up with a great return on your investment." But are we really? Five of Tom Green's wives are Colorado City girls who grew up to be even more welfare proficient. The five wives have in excess of thirty children. How many of them will grow up continuing to make babies and feed them with your tax dollars?

Dissidents from the FLDS disagree with Knudson. They claim that welfare in the FLDS has become a way of life. Zoellner found that the Cooperative Mercantile Exchange, the only grocery store in the twin cities, took in "$26,466.00 from the WIC food program in December 1997." WIC has so many demands from the FLDS that they must rent a $400 a month office from the town of Hildale.

The median age in Hildale is 13.1 years old.

Colorado City "received more than $1.8 million from the U.S. Department of Housing and Urban Development to pave its streets, upgrade its fire equipment and build a water-storage tank." Hildale received $94,000 to upgrade its fire station. An airport on the Arizona side received $2.8 million in government assistance. Dan Barlow, the mayor of Colorado City, denied that the airport was built to accommodate a chartered Learjet that would fly FLDS prophet Rulon Jeffs into town for Sunday meetings.

The fact of the matter is that after the landing strip was lengthened and improved, Rulon Jeffs, who liked to fly, took advantage of the improvement and on occasion chartered a lear jet to transport him to Colorado City. Barlow is correct in that the airport was not improved to accommodate Rulon Jeffs.

From taxpayers point of view, not only have things *not* improved since 1998, they have gotten worst. The twin cities of Colorado City and Hildale have not ceased to be fertile ground for investigative reporters looking for FLDS-controlled, government financial irregularities.

John Dougherty of the *Phoenix New Times* conducted a six month probe into FLDS financial practices and come up with an "array of unethical actions by the FLDS-controlled school board, district administrators and school principals."

"The investigation included an extensive review of thousands of pages of school district credit card records, travel vouchers, board minutes, district lease agreements and correspondence, all obtained under the Arizona Public Records Law."

The *Phoenix New Times* accused the Colorado City Unified School District, which has received state and federal aid in the amount of $4 million a year, of "operating primarily for the financial benefit of the FLDS church and for the personal enrichment of FLDS school district leaders."

On July 16, 2000, Warren Jeffs called the faithful FLDS members to separate themselves from associations, business, and doings with apostates. Members were forced to choose between the priesthood edict and their blood relatives – including wives, sons and daughters, who were not FLDS. Warren said, "Your only real family are the members of this Priesthood who are faithful to our Prophet."

This commandment compelled FLDS students, the majority of the student population (800), to stop attending public school and withdraw to their homes and be home-taught. This left only the kids and teachers of the Second Ward (Centennial Park). But FLDS school board administrators *still had control of school district funds*, which amounted to millions of dollars.

The *Phoenix New Times* investigation also turned up "prolific travel expenses, including the purchase of a $220,000 aircraft and the use of district credit cards for personal expenses."

The Colorado City school district has an annual budget of $5 million for a community of 5000 where there are "100 employees for 300 students, a 3 to 1 student to employee ratio." The average Mohave County employee ratio is one employee per 25 students. Pursuant to a state law that protects school districts from sudden declining student attendance, "Colorado City has received more than $3 million since July 2000 in state funds for phantom students who were withdrawn from the school by religious decree." Although student attendance dramatically dropped, employee numbers stayed the same.

Superintendent Alvin Barlow has accrued over $5000 of personal expenses he has not repaid dating back to July 2001. Another questionable expense is a $20,000 expenditure since January 2003 to operate a Cessna 210 aircraft, not to mention extravagant trips and hotel bills supposedly on school business, like an "accountability academy" meeting in San Diego.

The whole Colorado City school district mess has been turned over to the Arizona State Auditor General's Office, the State Superintendent of Public Instruction, and the Mohave County Superintendent of Schools. It will be interesting to see what develops, if anything. The tax base of Colorado City is far below towns of equal size. Consequently, a large portion of school funds comes from taxpayers outside Colorado City.

The situation in Colorado City is not unlike that of Tom Green's Order of Saint Michael. Colorado City is a privately owned religious community dependent upon government assistance. The real government of Colorado City is a priesthood theocracy *that uses federal and state monies to fortify its power over FLDS members.*

The administration of the Colorado City school district has apparently been trusted with millions of dollars to spend as they like with very little or no accountability, which in the eyes of taxpayers has resulted in bleeding the beast on a massive scale.

The Kingston polygamist group is considered to be the wealthiest of all the organized groups at the tune of $150 million. You would think that with all their money, especially the leadership, they would be above filching public welfare. But not so. In 1985 the leader of the Kingston Clan, John Ortell Kingston, was sued by the State of Utah for massive welfare fraud. It seems that Kingston's four wives and twenty-nine children had collected hundreds of thousands of dollars in public assistance over a ten year period. Kingston, whose personal assets were estimated at $70 million, never admitted guilt but settled with the state for $250,000.

According to Rowenna Erickson, co-founder of Tapestry Against Polygamy, Ortell Kingston taught that the Kingstons paid so much in taxes that they were entitled to get back what they could through welfare. It was like a return on their investment. Rowenna said that it is a safe assumption that many more Kingstons are filching the welfare system. She said that Paul Kingston, the current leader, has at least thirty wives.

The Kingston women have one other ploy they use to get government assistance. It's a day care program called Alliance for Children, where the government gives back so much money per child. Consequently, children are moved around between day care centers like Chinese checkers. What the government doesn't know is that they are probably reimbursing the same child as many as two and three times.

And what else have we learned? In November 2003 we learned from a documentary by ABC 15 News, Station NFWS Arizona television, that in one year the FLDS received $8 million in state and federal assistance while only generating $72,000 in taxes. $2.3 million was consumed in food stamps, $5 million in heath care, $660,000 in other government assistance. The more children polygamous families produce, the more government assistance they collected. It is not uncommon for women to give birth to as many as fourteen children.

How does a government bring about a change of attitude in the minds of all these children who know nothing about how to survive in today's world on their own, how to make the money to finance their own lives? To learn that one works for what one wants and needs. To be a self-supporting citizen of this great country. That is the question to be answered. And it will only begin when your tax dollars no longer support them.

Chapter Eight

Authority versus Love in Mormon Fundamentalism

The role of romantic love as a bonding agent between husband and wife in plural marriages was conspicuously absent in 19th century Mormonism, just as love among many of today's polygamist families is not a factor. In fact, such love between the husband and a plural wife could complicate a plural relationship. It should also be noted that not so long ago, romantic love was nice to have but not essential as women looked for men who could provide for and protect a family, and do so with kindness.

Rowenna Erickson of Tapestry Against Polygamy said, "When a plural wife is sealed to a husband in the FLDS or Kingston Group, and in many cases the Allred Group, love is not a prerequisite, or even an expectation. The binding component that welds the marriage, the bonding agent that ties the woman to her husband, is not love, but the *sealing authority* – in other words, the Fundamentalist priesthood. All elements that make for a good marriage, love, security, respect, equality, are subordinate to the power of the priesthood."

In many respects the wife becomes the "property" of the priesthood, and what the priesthood gives, the priesthood can take away. The relationship of the husband to the wife is a stewardship (and maybe even temporary) because the priesthood has the power to take the wife from one man and give her to another. In essence she is married to the priesthood.

In addressing the question of divorce or when a woman can leave her husband, the late Rulon Jeffs, president of the FLDS, recorded the following:

"If a woman can find a man holding the keys of the priesthood with higher power and authority than her husband, and he is disposed to take her, he can do so, otherwise she has got to remain where she is. To repeat, first, if a man forfeits his covenants with a wife, or wives, (by) becoming unfaithful to his God, and his priesthood, that wife or wives are free from him without a bill of divorcement. Second, if a woman claims protection at the hands of a man, possessing more power in the priesthood and higher keys, if he is disposed to rescue her and has obtained the consent of her husband to make her his wife, he can do so without bill of divorcement.[23]

The above was taken by Rulon from a sermon given by Brigham Young. Notice that he does not address unfaithfulness to the wife, only to priesthood, and it is the prophet who decides when the husband is unfaithful to his God or priesthood.

All of the organized polygamist groups today follow the same divorce and rescue procedure. But when it comes to rescuing a woman, a man is more apt to initiate a "higher priesthood rescue" than a woman. The rescue is usually contingent upon influence, or lack of influence, with that group's prophet, and not some misdeed. And the provision that states "consent of her husband" is not always followed and when it is followed, it is usually by way of coercion.

James D. Harmston, prophet of the True & Living Church has probably made more of the Doctrine of Rescue than the other prophets. Cindy Stewart, co-plaintiff in a lawsuit against Harmston, was transplanted from one family to another. While married to one of Harmston's apostles, she was in a position to obtain inside information about Harmston's method of rescue. She said that when a new family came into the group and the wife was pretty, Harmston and his apostles would look her over and decide if she ought to be *rescued*, and by whom.

Priesthood inclusion in the marriage relationship doesn't

mean that love can't exit among polygamist families. And speaking of love, while a member of Apostolic United Brethren, I observed some outstanding polygamist women who were excellent mothers. These mothers loved their children passionately and in many ways sacrificed for their children just as dramatically as monogamous mothers. Polygamist families are generally larger, money is scarce and, because polygamist fathers are often gone for extended periods of time, the mothers, out of necessity, often assume the role of both mother and father.

"When I say there is a lack of love in polygamist marriages," said Rowenna Erickson, "I'm referring to the lack of love at the time the woman is sealed to the man. It is not love that brings the man and woman together. It is the principle of plural marriage. When a Kingston man mentions love, he means sex. There is no such thing as romantic love, the kind of love you see in monogamous marriages. The relationship between the husband and the plural wife is ... well, mechanical, no emotion at all."

It would appear that lack of love is intrinsic in other polygamist groups, at least with the polygamists of Colorado City. Rodney Parker, an attorney for the FLDS, in a letter to Attorney General Mark Shurtleff, has been quoted as saying: "Although their model of marriage by revelation runs counter to traditional notions of romantic love and marriage, the model works for them because they have confidence in it." However, according to the anti-polygamist organization Help The Child Brides, the FLDS method works for them because the coercive power of Warren Jeffs tells them to make it work.

Rulon Jeffs in *Purity in the New and Everlasting Covenant of Marriage* referred to the "model" mentioned by Parker as, "...the placement system that has been instituted by the holy Priesthood, through President Barlow and President Johnson." Jeffs considered it a sin for young boys and girls to fraternize or seek each other out as husband and wife without priesthood supervision.

"It's sad," said Erickson, "that a third or fourth wife, even though she may give birth to several children, may spend the rest of her life without experiencing the warm affection, passion, and adoration experienced by monogamous women. She may never know what it's like to receive a birthday card, a box of candy or a red rose on her anniversary. In the Kingston Group," she said, "the young people are taught that such things are frivolous and unbecoming. There are no green grass or flowers in the yards of some of the Kingston leaders. If there's a tree, it's a weed tree that made it on its own. In the Kingston Clan, it's a black and white existence for the women, no color in their lives. For the men, it's making money, saving money, and sex." She had tears in her eyes when she said, "There are actually teenage children in the Kingston Clan who don't know who their father is."

"In fact," said Rowenna, "as a plural wife you work at *not* loving your husband." More tears started welling in her eyes and her voice cracked with emotion. She choked back the tears and said, "You learn *not* to love your husband because when he goes to bed with another wife, it hurts too much...."

There are three kinds of power – the power of presence, the power of communication, and the power of position. The ideal relationship is a balance of these three powers with love. But what happens when we apply this to plural relationships in Colorado City or the Kingston Clans?

The power of presence is the power of the priesthood which is ubiquitous and omnipresent. Priesthood presence is the governing power that dictates everything from the way a woman will dress to how she will coiffeur her hair. The policemen that patrol the streets in Colorado City and Hildale are priesthood police like the Taliban, making sure the people conform to priesthood standards in their homes as well as on the streets.

The power of communication is the voice of the priesthood that dictates the role of the wife and the role of the husband. The woman listens to the voice of the priesthood at Sunday meetings, and hears it again at home as the husband articulates his authority.

The power of position is manifest in the theocratic chain of command. The prophet stands in the place of God. The priesthood is his power — his army, the muscle that enforces the priesthood edicts. That muscle trickles down to the husband who reins supreme over the wife. It is the wife's lot to obey the husband, who obeys the priesthood, who obeys the prophet. Position is everything in a polygamist marriage from first wife, favorite wife to secondary wife, etc.

When I was a deputy sheriff I came face to face with Rulon Jeffs during a drowning that occurred near his home in the mouth of Little Cottonwood Canyon. I said to him, "I have heard that in Colorado City, young girls are forced into unwanted marriages?"

He looked me straight in the eye and said, "When a girl reaches marital age she presents herself before the priesthood to see what family the Lord wants her to enter. She does it voluntarily. There is no forcing of girls in Colorado City."

However, that is not what the runaway women from the FLDS say, and they all agree. In the FLDS the priesthood decides what man a girl will marry. She has no say in the matter. Her husband may already have three or four wives. He may even have daughters older than his new child bride. That makes no difference because "God" has decided who she shall marry, and to disobey God will put her exaltation at risk.

Five of Tom Green's wives were born and raised in the FLDS. The adult wives Beth and June married Tom as a means of escaping Colorado City. June's daughter, Shirley, told the author that she chose to marry Tom so she would not be forced into a marriage with someone she despised. LeeAnn and Linda grew up there also.

It is therefore "obedience to priesthood" that binds the wife to the husband. Once united, it is the duty of the husband to feed her, clothe her, and keep her in a perpetual state of pregnancy. By having as many children as her body will tolerate, the wife fulfills the commandment to multiply and replenish the earth. In that regard, it is not unusual for some women to give birth to as many as fourteen children. And besides raising the children, some women are required to work in various priesthood businesses to help support the family.

Chapter Nine

Legal Issues and Four Attitudes Towards Polygamy

When President Abraham Lincoln signed the Morrill Anti-Bigamy Law on July 8, 1862, his thoughts were primarily occupied with the rebellion in the South. Lincoln still supported the Republican platform of 1856, which declared that slavery and polygamy were the "twin relics of barbarism," but in 1862 he was not inclined to fight a political war on two fronts. Congress had given Lincoln a weapon with which to combat polygamy, but he chose not to use it. In reflecting back upon the stress Lincoln must have been under, attempting to find a political solution that would avoid a civil war, it is hard to find fault with his solution on polygamy, which was no solution.

And ever since the 1953 raid on the polygamist community of Short Creek by Arizona Governor Pyle, state and county officials in Utah and Arizona have let the polygamy issue alone.

Four Attitudes

The attitudes of the people in Utah and Arizona towards polygamists vary from sympathy, envy, and embarrassment to outrage. A legislator or elected official, faced with the dilemma to act or not act, *must* take public attitude into consideration. His decision may be predicated upon how he perceives public attitude *or* it can be based upon his own inner convictions. A public official's career is dependent upon votes and the ability to get his message before the voting public. All of these things must be taken into consideration, including how his actions will be viewed by persons and institutions of political influence. True or false, most people in Utah and Arizona believe that leaders in the LDS Church wield immense political influence, and politicians do not want to embarrass the Church or its members.

One example: In order for Utah to achieve statehood, a provision was put into the State Constitution "forever" banning the practice of plural marriage. But in 1999, Utah State Legislator David Zolman, R-Taylorsville, proposed that the constitutional ban on polygamy be removed. He also thought that the legislature should apologize to the people of Colorado City for the 1953 raid on polygamist families authorized by the governor of Arizona, which made national headlines and tore apart families. The Legislature was not impressed. Nevertheless, Zolman received a lot of publicity from *The Salt Lake Tribune* over his egalitarian concerns for polygamists. But a year later, Zolman failed in his bid for reelection. His outspoken sympathies for Mormon Fundamentalists, no matter how justified, cost him his political career.

Sympathy

Even though polygamy is no longer practiced by members of the LDS Church, plural marriage or celestial marriage is still a valid LDS religious belief. This contradiction can't help but create a quandary in the minds of faithful Latter-day Saints. Joseph Smith, the revered prophet and founder of Mormonism, was himself a polygamist. For three decades plural marriage (1852 - 1890) was the axis around which Mormonism revolved. All the leading men of the LDS Church – Brigham Young, John Taylor, Orson Pratt, Wilford Woodruff – just to name a few, had taken plural wives. Although only a small fraction of the Church membership practiced polygamy, it is a safe bet that at least a third, if not half, of Utah natives (and many in Arizona) are the second, third or fourth generation progeny of polygamist ancestors. Some pundits think the percentage could be as high as two-thirds.

Regardless, a few of Utah's and Arizona's more notable citizens can trace their heritage to respected and valiant Mormons who had plural wives; for example, former Utah Governor Mike Leavitt, who was recently confirmed as administrator of the Environmental Protection Agency (EPA).[24]

A family tree with polygamist ancestors is no big deal in Utah. "The big deal," says retired Captain David Bishop, Salt Lake County Sheriff's Office, "is that polygamists have been driven underground. Under the cover of isolation and secrecy polygamist leaders tend to become oppressive, abusive, and misuse their religious authority."

Bishop, an accomplished student of Mormonism, is the great grandson of Mahonri Moreancumer Bishop, and can trace his polygamist ancestors in four different directions: Bishop, Whipple, Harris, and Brunson. Bishop is not ashamed of his heritage. He believes that if polygamy were decriminalized, it would tend to neutralize the abuse that is found in the FLDS and Kingston Clan. A comparison between the FLDS and Apostolic United Brethren (AUB) tends to support Bishop's hypothesis. The FLDS is a closed, isolated, and impudent society. By comparison, AUB is open and accommodating with very little abuse and no "child bride" forced marriages.

Many in Utah and Arizona share Bishop's opinion but are circumspect in where and how they convey their opinions due to the fear of political or ecclesiastical repercussions, which is unfortunate. Over the years, many brilliant and productive men and women have emanated from the loins of polygamists as exemplified by the historical works of author Juanita Brooks.

United States Senator from Utah, Orrin Hatch, has been quoted as saying: "I happen to feel that a legitimate argument can be made that the 1879 Reynolds vs. United States was wrongly decided, and its progeny since." (Reynolds vs. United States was a supreme court decision that, in essence, removed plural marriage from the realm of religious freedom.)

In responding to *The Salt Lake Tribune* inquiry reported October 27, 2003, Senator Hatch said that a Supreme Court decision that tossed a Texas law banning consensual sodomy by homosexuals may also invalidate Utah's constitutional ban on polygamy and other state laws prohibiting incest and bigamy.

"The legal argument is there," the Senate Judiciary Committee chairman says of the precedent the high court set in a June ruling that the anti-sodomy statute unconstitutionally infringed on individual rights. "The current Supreme Court ruled that whether a majority of the public opposes a particular practice as immoral, it's not sufficient reason for upholding a law prohibiting that practice." (This 2003 decision seems to be a reversal of the 1879 decision.)

In reviewing the Reynolds case, the Supreme Court (at that time) said that "while they cannot interfere with mere religious belief and opinions, they may with practices,"and therefore "provided that plural marriage shall not be allowed." The Court went on to say: "To permit this (plural marriage) would be to make the professed doctrines of religious belief superior to the laws of the land and in effect to permit every citizen to become a law unto himself."

George Reynolds, who had been convicted of bigamy, had appealed to the United States Supreme Court on the grounds that polygamy was part of the LDS religion and should be protected by the First Amendment. The court disagreed in an 1879 decision and upheld the territorial court. The LDS Church disagreed with the Supreme Court and Gustive O. Larson attempts to tell why the Church disagreed. Larson compared the court's decision with the rational of the LDS Church, in other words, he weighed one against the other. In reading Larson, I get the impression that he possibly felt like Senator Hatch, that the Reynolds decision was "wrongly decided." The Morrill Law was designed to punish and prevent the practice of polygamy in the Territories of the United States and to disapprove and annul certain acts of the territorial legislature of Utah.

Historian Gustive O. Larson, author of *The "Americanization" of Utah for Statehood,* weighed the 1879 Reynolds decision with the position of the LDS Church:

This reasoning (Reynolds) was based upon the Jeffersonian interpretation that while freedom of belief is inviolate, actions which result from those beliefs may be subject to regulation depending upon their effect on society – whether they are destructive of peace, purity, and good order. With this reasoning the Saints could find no fault, but they claimed a weakness in the decision on the ground that "celestial marriage," as they called it, was not identical with bigamy, upon which view the court apparently based its decision. *Plural marriage as practiced by the Mormons was not a civil contract but a religious ceremony, and they challenged the Court to specify wherein their particular practice was harmful to society or a threat to public peace and good order....*

As practiced by the Saints, polygamy required the assumption of marital responsibilities by the husband and was based upon *knowledge and consent of the first wife* and with equity governing the relations of the polygamous household. The women understood and accepted the doctrine that they would share the spiritual rewards of their common husband in the life to come. Thus, argued the Mormons, polygamy was definitely a part of their religion, and as it resulted in no harm to society, it claimed protection under the First Amendment of the United States Constitution.[25]   (Italics added)

In response to the Reynolds decision, the polygamist women of Utah sent a memorial to Congress:

> And moreover we, your petitioners, hereby testify that we are happy in our homes and satisfied with our marriage relations and desire no change.

The position of polygamist women then was reinforced by the fact that Utah women were the first to be granted the right of suffrage. In many ways the women spearheading the pro-polygamy movement today is a re-enactment of proponents of yesterday, with the exception of two things.

The *assumption is made* that "celestial marriage" today is about family and consent – consent of the first wife, and consent of the plural wife. Clearly, in some of the Fundamentalist groups, "consent" is forced. In the FLDS when young girls reach childbearing age, they are summoned before the priesthood and told what family they shall enter. The marriage might occur at that very moment with no warning to the young girl, or the next day. The girls are not asked if they consent, nor is the first wife asked to consent. If a young girl takes it upon herself to resist the marriage, she may be imprisoned for weeks, months or years, like Flora Jessop, until she consents. Or the girl may be rendered incognito by erecting a barrier to all outside influences including brothers, sisters, and mother as in the case of Ruby Jessop, Flora's little sister.

Coerced marriages and incestuous marriages are not harmonious with *public peace and good order*. According to Flora Jessop, incest is as much a problem in the FLDS as it is in the Kingston Clan. She stated that in one family a child was born with no legs or arms. In the same family, a child was born with no fingers. She blames incest.

Assuming Senator Hatch is correct in his interpretation of the law (that 1879 Reynolds was wrongly decided), the FLDS and Kingston Clan are not helping those who would like to see polygamy decriminalized and removed from the bigamy statute.

Nevertheless, depending upon the jurisdiction, a policy not to intervene between consenting adults is already in force. Most Utah law enforcement agencies do not have the manpower or inclination to devote time towards bigamy cases *unless another felony is associated*, like incest or child rape. And even then some jurisdictions don't bother with bigamy.

For example, District Attorney David Yokom, Salt Lake City, successfully prosecuted David Ortell Kingston for Incest. He could have also charged Kingston with bigamy but chose not to. Yokom did not add bigamy to the incest charge of Jeremy Ortell Kingston who pled guilty October 30, 2003.

Law enforcement officers throughout the State of Utah, including Mark Shurtleff, have repeatedly been quoted as saying, "It is not about religion, but about abuse." Even Flora Jessop, one of the most vocal activists of Help The Child Brides, is firm in her conviction, and said, "It's about abuse, not religion." Flora told the author, "I'm not attacking the *practice* of polygamy, I'm attacking the men in polygamy who are abusing young girls and boys." Flora has many relatives still living at Colorado City who she says are good people.

Is it really not about religion?
There is nothing in the plural marriage revelation, the 132nd Section of the Doctrine & Covenants, that condones incest or forced marriages.

The FLDS priesthood considers it their priesthood duty to *control* the marriages of their members. They believe their authority over conjugal prerogatives should be protected by the First Amendment, even though their conjugal directives might be in conflict with the civil rights of young girls. In the Mormon Fundamentalist lexicon, the laws of God take precedence over the laws of the land. In the FLDS a young girl is not given her free will to choose or reject plural marriage. The only way she can avoid a plural relationship is to run away.

Retired Sheriff's Captain David Bishop points out that actions are crimes either "malum prohibitum," because the legislature says so, or "malum en se," because the act is evil in and of itself. Polygamy is made a crime under the bigamy statute by virtue of an act of the legislature because polygamy is not acceptable to the majority.

Consequently, an act of legislature has turned an entire society of people into criminals.

Is it the marriage ceremony or the cohabiting that makes polygamists criminals? According to the bigamy statute it is both. But what do we have if we remove the marriage ceremony from the equation?

By putting the "marriage ceremony" aside (the ceremony being synonymous with religion), we can look at polygamy as a moral issue and not a criminal act. There are hundreds of examples where prominent men have taken mistresses, and the mistresses themselves have become famous. Influential married men have cohabited with their mistresses and even sired children, their dalliance winked at, and in the absence of a marriage ceremony they have not been prosecuted.

Josephine was first a paramour and after she married Napoleon, took a lover on the side. Bathsheba was David's mistress until he arranged for Uriah's death. Numerous books have been written about the fifteen mistresses of King Charles II. The infamous mistress of Louis XV, Madame DePompadour, or Madame DuBarry, has forever captured the attention of writers around the world. Our own Thomas Jefferson has been linked to Sally Hemings, his purported Black mistress. John Barrymore had Mary Astor, Charlie Chaplin had Joan Barry, Thomas Wolfe had Aline Bernstein, Henry Ford had Evangeline Cote Dahlinger, Peter Abelard had Heloise.[26] The list goes on and on, an aggregate of movie stars, politicians, poets, gangsters, writers, statesmen, industrialists, and philandering American presidents like Kennedy and Clinton. But when the Fundamentalist men honored their mistresses with a marriage ceremony, it became a crime.

You would think that polygamist leaders would be in favor of decriminalization, *but that is not the case.* Owen A. Allred, leader of the second largest polygamist group has publically declared his opposition to decriminalization. He is afraid that if polygamy were no longer a crime people would start practicing polygamy haphazardly and the sacredness would be lost. He suggested that if the state would place him in charge of polygamist marriages, *he would make sure* it was lived properly. For Allred, polygamy is a celestial calling and must be lived within celestial parameters.

Anti-polygamists say that Allred's opposition to decriminalization is founded on profit and not religion. Polygamy is more profitable when it's against the law. In essence, what Allred is doing is bootlegging polygamy. According to Fundamentalist doctrine, in order for a polygamist union to be efficacious it must be sealed by one having authority. Allred claims to be that one and only man. But before Allred will grant authority, the husband must acknowledge that Owen A. Allred is the one and only prophet of God, and pay tithes to Allred. In other words, it costs money to obtain a spiritually legal, plural wife, ten percent of your gross income.

Envy

Tom Green had five young, pretty, energetic wives that were fully committed to the polygamist lifestyle. Tom knew he was envied by other polygamists, and was convinced he was envied by most monogamous males. But it wasn't the responsibility of supporting five wives and thirty kids that on-lookers envied, it was the thought of consensual sex with five lovely ladies.

The one and only edition of the pro-polygamy magazine *Mormon Focus* featured three beautiful women, sister-wives, on the cover. Why were these particular beauties selected? To show that plural wives are not all ugly? Or did the editor pick these pretty gals knowing that they would stimulate envy?

A rich man built a mansion conspicuously high on top of a hill. When asked why he picked the top of a hill, he said it was so he could view the valley below. But in his heart, he wanted to be envied by the people below.

If I have heard it once, I have heard it fifty times, a monogamous man saying, "What would I do with four or five wives, I can't handle one?" But the smile on his face and twinkle in eyes says he wouldn't mind trying.

It's doubtful that even a few monogamous men are foolish enough to admit to envying a polygamist, but I know they do because their pithy remarks give them away.

Embarrassment

In the last decade Mormon polygamists have brought more

bad publicity to the State of Utah than even the bribery, fraud, and conspiracy allegations over obtaining the 2002 Winter Olympic Games. Polygamy is called Utah's "dirty little secret."

In 1998 the country was shocked when a polygamist father beat his sixteen-year-old daughter senseless for refusing to continue as the fifteenth wife of her uncle. In 2002, Tom Green, the most affable polygamist of them all, threatened to rival the Winter Olympics as media from around the world sidestepped the games and doubled up with a story about the infamous Tom Green and Utah's bizarre polygamists. In 2002, the unprecedented kidnaping and subsequent extraordinary rescue of Elizabeth Smart captured the hearts of the nation. After awhile the religious aspects of her kidnaping were set aside, and the media focused on Elizabeth's parents, their stress and undaunted hope and faith that Elizabeth was alive.

At this writing, Elizabeth's abductor, Brian David Mitchell, has not yet come to trial. Psychologists evaluating Mitchell are divided. The defense psychologists say Mitchell is insane and should not go to trial. The prosecution psychologists say Mitchell is perfectly sane and should stand trail, which is no surprise. The contradiction between defense and state psychologists in criminal cases has been acted out thousands of times.

If Mitchell goes to trial, the media will once again focus on the religious factor that motivated the kidnaping. But as it was in the Tom Green bigamy trial, the defense will more than likely be prohibited from using religion as a defense. But that won't stop the media from digging deeper into the LDS Church polygamist past.

Should The Church of Jesus Christ of Latter-day Saints be embarrassed by the criminal antics of Mormon fundamentalists?

Tom Green wanted to use religion as a defense and sent a warning to David Leavitt that he intended to subpoena President Gordon B. Hinckley. But Tom was prohibited by the Judge because the United States Supreme Court had ruled that the practice of polygamy was not protected by the First Amendment.

When Attorney General Mark Shurtleff says his probing into

the Fundamentalist Church is not about religion, but about abuse, should we disregard the fact that all of these criminal acts have a common denominator, Mormon Fundamentalism? Would it be a blessing in disguise if Brian David Mitchell and his wife were adjudicated insane and there was no trial, and no media feeding frenzy? It would certainly be much easier for Elizabeth.

There is no question that polygamy has brought a bright blush to the face of Utah, there is no doubt about it. And what do we do when we are embarrassed? We either get mad or pretend it didn't happen.

So how are Utahns and Arizonans reacting to Attorney General Mark Shurtleff's probing into the illegal affairs of the FLDS? Is his involvement exacerbating a hopeless, insolvable problem? Or does Utah finally have a man with the integrity to shove politics aside and use his judicial authority to right a wrong?

Outrage

It started in earnest in 1998 with dissident women from the polygamist subculture. Nightmares and heartaches brought them together and they formed Tapestry Against Polygamy. The women from Tapestry marched back and forth between the Governor and the Attorney General's offices with stories of child abuse, wife abuse, and tyranny, but were met with only token success (not unlike victims of domestic violence from monogamous marriages did some years ago). Eventually they caught the ear of *The Salt Lake Tribune* and things started to happen, little things at first, but positive things. Finally, they had a forum where they could vent their outrage.

Soon after, dissidents in Southern Utah rallied with child protection activists and started their own campaign. The target was the FLDS, believed to be the most tyrannical and oppressive of the polygamist groups. The forced marriage of fourteen-year-old Ruby Jessop brought outraged people together and Ruby became the Internet poster girl of another anti-polygamy group calling themselves Help The Child Brides. Soon, the telephone wires sang with e-mails speeding back and forth between Tapestry and people of Help The Child Brides.

According to Flora Jessop, Ruby's older sister, Southern Utah activists could not get the Washington County Sheriff or the County Attorney to take them seriously. They had even less luck with Arizona elected officials.

It wasn't until *The Spectrum,* Southern Utah's St. George based newspaper, began taking notice that things started to happen. The outrage spread to *The Arizona Republic* and the *Phoenix New Times.* At about the same time Utah Attorney General Mark Shurtleff became actively involved, which seemed to inspire new interest in torpid elected officials in Southern Utah and Arizona. The Colorado City based polygamist group suddenly became an election issue in Arizona. By then it was a common assumption that the child abuse in the FLDS was real. The political issue was not who had done the most to combat abuse, but who had done the least. Both the *Republic* and *New Times* demanded answers.

The continuous probing by Utah investigator Ron Barton and investigative journalists in Arizona uncovered information that not only were unlawful child marriages a recurring problem but that Colorado City officials may have grossly misused public money. Finally, taxpayers were outraged. And for the proponents of Help The Child Brides, their outrage had boiled to full maturity.

What is the prevailing attitude of people in Utah and Arizona towards the doctrine of polygamy and the people who practice plural marriage? It is one of tolerance and ambiguity. It is my guess that the majority of citizens in Utah and Arizona would say arrest the bad ones and leave the good ones alone. Except where tax money is being misused, most people seem content to let the anti-polygamists, the pro-polygamists, and the Attorney General work out solutions.

Chapter Ten

Are There Realistic Solutions for Polygamy Abuses

In looking for solutions to the polygamy abuse problem, it must be acknowledged that there is a valid Mormon Fundamentalist subculture with at least 30,000 members. This subculture is well established and here to stay. It doesn't matter whether one agrees with plural marriage, the practice is so widespread that government can't even begin to enforce the bigamy statute, even if it wanted to.

It is not against the law to believe that plural marriage is essential to a celestial exaltation, but the practice of plural marriage is presently against the law.

The fundamentalist subculture is divided into three main groups with several smaller groups and a large population of independent polygamists who are not organized. Most of the civil rights violations, forced marriages, and welfare abuses seem to be concentrated in two groups, the FLDS and Kingston group.

The Utah legislature has passed laws in an attempt to combat abuse among the polygamists. It raised the age from fourteen to sixteen that a minor girl can marry with parental consent. The legislature has defined *marriage* and made it unlawful to perform an "unlawful marriage." If a polygamist prophet should perform a plural marriage with a minor, it is a felony. A man commits a felony if he has sex with a minor and he is ten years older than the minor.

In Arizona the age of legal consent is eighteen. If sixteen or seventeen, the consent of at least one parent is required. If fifteen years of age or younger, the law requires an order signed by the

Juvenile Court Judge of the Superior Court. And Arizona does not ban polygamy as such, but does have a bigamy law.

Civil lawsuits are used as partial solutions by exposing the inner workings of the polygamist groups. This tactic worked when Virginia Hill sued Owen A. Allred , and when Kaziah May Hancock sued James D. Harmston.

The Arizona Republic reported on October 15, 2003, "Wives suing to bring end to abuse under polygamy" by Judy Nichols:

> "Arizona Sen. Linda Binder (R-Lake Havasu City) who represents the area including Colorado City, said civil suits worked in attacking the Aryan Nation and seeking justice from the Catholic Church. 'You have to cut the head off the snake,' Binder said. 'And that's the money. There are estimates that the (fundamentalist church) has $400 million. I'd love to see the victims get that money to educate and relocate the women and children, give them a fresh start in life.'... 'The men up there are fat and happy, smiling,' she said. 'They've got all the women they want, all the sex, and the government pays for their children.'"

The article further reported the attorneys general in both states are coming together to crack down on polygamy-related crimes. Arizona Attorney General Terry Goddard confirmed:

> "that he has a lawyer and an investigator looking full time into the polygamist community of Colorado City. . . . Officials in both states are looking into welfare fraud allegations. . ."

In August 2003, Mary Ann Kingston filed a suit against Paul Eldon Kingston, the leader of the Kingston Clan, and 241 other defendants. She is asking for a total of $110 million, which includes punitive, general, and special damages.

Mary Ann, now age twenty-two, is the sixteen-year-old girl who testified that she was coerced into a plural marriage with her uncle David Ortell Kingston, and was belt-whipped by her father John Daniel Kingston. David was convicted of incest and sent to prison, while John Daniel served twenty-eight weeks in jail for the whipping.

In the complaint, Mary Anne makes numerous allegations, some more interesting than others. Under the heading "The Order," which presumably means the belief system of the Kingston "religious order," the complaint states:

29. The Order involves a secret society of men and women that practice and promote polygamy, incest and the sexual abuse of young girls.

30. The Order permeates every aspect of the social, familial, and economic life of the Order Members.

40. Certain families within the Order are believed to carry the blood of ancient prophets, including Jesus Christ.

41. These families are usually given the authority of the "keys" of governing the Order.

42. The Kingston family has always held the primary rights of governance.

47. The young boys and girls are taught that incest is not wrong and is, in fact, a preferred practice to preserve a pure family bloodline originating from Jesus Christ.

48. The young girls expect to be told at an early age to whom they will marry by a male polygamist who has received "direction" from God for a particular young girl.

Under the heading, "Wedding," Mary Ann states the following:

63. Mary Ann's parents pressured her to accept the proposal.

65. On or about October 13, 1997, David Kingston proposed to Mary Ann that they get married on October 15, just 48 hours away.

66. David Kingston explained to Mary Ann that he had cleared the wedding with her mother, Paul Kingston, the Order's prophet, and David Kingston's brother. Mary Ann was emotionally devastated and believed she had no way out. She did not want to be married to David Kingston and be required to have sex with him and bear his children.

68. The day following, October 15, 1997, was the day of the wedding.

71. ...Mary Ann become David's fifteenth wife.

The complaint is broken down into twenty-six separate causes of action stemming from a coerced marriage, sexual abuse, assault, battery, intentional infliction of emotional distress and intentional infliction of emotional distress. Mary Ann hopes to draw into the action members and companies of "The Order" by showing that they either contributed to her abuse or could have prevented it.

The goals of the complaint are to seek damages, inflict punishment, and at the same time reveal as much as about the Order's bizarre beliefs as possible.

The Kingston policy of refraining from public comment prevents us from getting their side of the story. It has been because of Paul Kingston's reluctance to grant interviews that suggests to the public that the allegations must be true. However, a confidential source close to the Kingston hierarchy predicts that there will be numerous counter-suits, and remember that Paul Kingston has a law degree. The source also indicated that the defense will show that Mary Ann is not the innocent, virtuous victim that she purports to be. The source also hinted that newspapers in Las Vegas who have been depicting "The Order" as polygamists and abusers of women may be sued because the stories have caused The Order to lose good customers.

It has been reported that a Class-Action lawsuit against Warren Jeffs and the Colorado City FLDS has been filed in Canada by dissidents from the FLDS community of Bountiful, located on the Canadian side of the Canada-Idaho border. According to Vaughan Marshall, one of the lawyers helping to prepare the class-action suit, when government declines to prosecute fringe groups the last "bastion for the victims is civil court."

The Bountiful, Canada, community was once a solid FLDS enclave. But a split occurred when Warren Jeffs replaced Winston Blackmore as Bountiful's priesthood leader. The replacement resulted over conflicts of authority. Half of the community followed Blackmore while the other half has stayed loyal.

According to reliable sources, the Blackmore faction is much more open and liberal than the FLDS faction, much the same as the openness of Centennial Park. In *Leaving Bountiful, A Documentary Film*, written and directed by Helen Slinger, she reports "As spiritual leader of Bountiful, Blackmore had complete control over every aspect of life. He was church bishop, superintendent of the school, ran the businesses, edited the newspaper, and was even allowed by local child welfare authorities to share control of reporting of abuse allegations." (More can be read about this film on Help The Child Brides web site.)

At this writing, Utah Attorney General Mark Shurtleff has taken the lead in finding solutions to the polygamy abuse problem. The Utah Attorney General is pushing to decertify Hildale City policemen who have plural wives or who are refusing to enforce the law. The Peace Officer Standards and Training Council (POST) has voted "unanimously that bigamy is an offense that could end an officer's career," reported *The Salt Lake Tribune* in late 2003.

Other actions under consideration are decertifying public officials and revoking the Hildale City charter. These might be ruthless measures, but if the FLDS priesthood is receiving federal and state funds, and if there is evidence that the civil rights of young boys and girls are being violated, then these measures may be in order.

In spite of denials by Colorado City and Hildale mayors that there is no FLDS oppression in their communities, the signs are there. When a stranger enters town he is followed, the license number is taken and turned over to the local police. When investigators from the Attorney General's Office attempted to obtain the help of the Hildale police in serving subpoenas on Hildale citizens, the Hildale Police Chief hesitated. According to Chief Sam Roundy, it has always been *the function of the sheriff* to serve subpoenas. Roundy finally agreed to send one of his officers with the investigators to point out the persons to be served. However, *by that time*, the people who were to be served could not be found.

Utah and Arizona have discussed the possibility of erecting a court house, a safe house, or some other structure in or near Colorado City that will be useful in helping abused women. When Arizona suggested the building be in Colorado City, it rubbed against the feathers of Help The Child Brides.

To Mark Shurtleff's credit, he has consulted the opinion of historian Ben Bistline, who is undoubtedly the most credible and knowledgeable source of information when it comes to polygamy and Colorado City.

Ben Bistline is an energetic man in his early seventies who was raised in Colorado City. He was one of the men who opposed the one-man-rule of Rulon Jeffs and the strangle hold of the United Effort Plan (UEP). Ben has family and friends in both the FLDS and Centennial Park. He is not a polygamist, he is an active member of the LDS Church and serves on the stake high council.

One only has to read Ben's book *The Polygamists: A History of Colorado City, Arizona* to realize he knows more about the people, their motives, their family connections, their religion, their strengths, and their weaknesses than any other pundit. The history of Colorado City and its people, the conditions that drove devout Mormons to a desolate desert, is as dramatic and as important to Utah and Arizona history as the 1890 Manifesto banning polygamy. Ben's book is well organized and well written.

Ben has watched with apprehension as politicians and anti-polygamists have debated the issue of a safe house. I asked Ben what he thought should be done.

First, he said the police in both Colorado City and Hildale need to be decertified. The police are priesthood police and continually harass the kids who are not FLDS. Rodney Holm was one of the most abusive of those policemen who misused their authority. The priesthood police, he said, cannot be relied upon to enforce the law fairly. Colorado City Police Officer Rodney Holm was convicted in August 2003 of bigamy and unlawful sex with a minor he took as a "spiritual" wife. The sixteen-year-old girl was his third wife.

Ben suggested that a sheriff's substation be built near Hildale on BLM property, not UEP property, and manned by at least three peace officers, one of which should be a women, and one a state officer to balance out the lethargy shown by the Washington County Sheriff. Ben suggested a woman police officer because in the past, girls fleeing Colorado City have become romantically involved with their policemen helpers.

Ben said he would be surprised if more than one adult woman a year sought sanctuary at the substation, but there would be a lot of young people, more boys than girls. He said the girls could use the help in escaping priesthood-coerced marriages. Take away the UEP's power over property and their ability to evict people without reimbursement, then take away the priesthood's power to coerce marriages, and you will have a liberated community.

The question has been asked, why were the polygamist groups allowed to incorporate? The primary reason was economics, to let the polygamist communities provide their own services. Because of the isolation of Colorado City and Hildale, it seemed to make good economic sense. David Leavitt, who was the Juab County Attorney when Rocky Ridge was allowed to incorporate, said letting the polygamist groups provide their own services seemed like a good idea because it saved the county money.

Another novel solution is for government to enlist the cooperation of anti-polygamy activists and polygamy proponents in helping solve the problems of abuse in the subculture, and the Utah Attorney General has moved in that direction, but not without problems.

In Salt Lake City there are two spirited groups of women, one for and the other against the practice of polygamy. Tapestry Against

Polygamy is the opposing voice and has the eyes and ears of the media. The authors of the self published pro-polygamy book *Voices In Harmony,* now calling themselves "Principle Voices," represent the proponents of polygamy. According to Anne Wilde, these ladies, Wilde, Mary Ann Watson, Mary Bachelor, and Linda Kelch have quickly earned the respect of influential members of the Attorney General's Office and the media.

According to Anne Wilde, their goal is to make government aware that not all people living plural marriage are lawbreakers and that not all women and children are being abused. Anne acknowledges that yes, there are serious problems that exist in the subculture. But the problems are not as widespread as the media has made it appear. Anne said that a secondary goal is to decriminalize, not legalize, but to decriminalize plural marriage between consenting adults. Like David Bishop, she believes that labeling polygamists as criminals drives them underground where women and children are more apt to be abused.

Anne and her co-author Mary Bachelor attended the August 2003 summit held by the Utah Attorney General at St. George. About 100 women from Centennial Park unexpectedly showed up at the Summit, and Anne and Mary became acquainted with them.

Working together, they then arranged for a private meeting in which the Attorney Generals from Utah and Arizona could meet and see for themselves that the women of Centennial Park were happy with their lifestyle, were opposed to child bride marriages, and were not welfare dependent.

Anne said the meeting was a huge success. Seven ladies from Centennial Park gave presentations in defense of their lifestyle. According to Anne, when the presentations were over Mark Shurtleff addressed the gathering and said that he now had a different concept of the polygamist lifestyle, that not all polygamists were the same, that there were women who actually not only preferred the lifestyle, but were very happy.

The Utah Attorney General then invited Anne to participate in discussions concerning alternative resources in helping women and children who want to exit the polygamist lifestyle. Vicky Prunty of Tapestry Against Polygamy was also invited. However, when Prunty learned that Anne Wilde had been invited she sent a letter to Mark Shurtleff refusing to sit at the same table with Anne.

Prunty said, "... bringing in a representative from the *pro-polygamy* community to discuss ways to help individuals *fleeing polygamy* causes problems and a major conflict of interest." Tapestry's position is that the practice of polygamy is evil in and of itself, is a crime, and should remain a crime. Prunty claims that polygamy proponents have compared them with the Klu Klux Klan. She believes it is an insult to expect members of Tapestry to sit side by side with polygamy proponents.

Anne Wilde denies that she has ever referred to Tapestry as Klu Klux Klan and wished Vicky would reconsider. Anne states that her role at the meeting would be restricted to helping find solutions for women who want to leave polygamy, not promoting polygamy. Because of her knowledge of the subculture, she believes that her presence would bring balance to the thinking. She believes that if the Attorney General is aware of all aspects of the fundamentalist subculture, he will be in a better position to institute solutions and find resources for those wanting to leave the subculture.

On November 21, 2003, *The Salt Lake Tribune* printed an editorial entitled, "Building a Bridge." The editorial chastised Tapestry (TAP) for comparing Anne Wilde with a "rapist in rape-crisis counseling," and said Tapestry was like a "small child that picks up its marbles and stomps home."

The editorial went on to say: But what Wilde can bring to the enterprise is valuable perspective and the experience of a woman who has not turned against polygamy. As an insider, she knows firsthand the backgrounds of those the group would be helping. She, better than those outside the polygamous community, can get the word to others that help is available, and women considering leaving polygamy would be more comfortable confiding in someone who understands them.

"Sadly, TAP's unwillingness to participate could be a setback for a project aimed at helping women abandon plural marriage – which is just what TAP would like to encourage."

The Tribune ended the editorial by encouraging Tapestry to "reconsider, and to become an 'active partner' with the state in building that bridge."

The *Tribune* article is *an example of government and media misunderstanding of the complexities* of the polygamy problem.

The Attorney General doesn't need either Tapestry or Principle Voices to involve other resource agencies. Tapestry and Voices have no resources like beds, food, clothes, or houses. What they do offer are their experiences, emotions, good intentions, and the desire for recognition.

If the goal is to help girls and women who want to leave polygamist communities, then what the Attorney General needs is a neutral party. Anne Wilde will be no more welcome in the FLDS and the Kingston Group than Vicky Prunty. It doesn't matter how experienced Anne Wilde might be, or how true she is to the principle of plural marriage. If she attempts to assist an unhappy plural wife out of the FLDS she will be demonized, because it's not about happiness, fairness or religion, it's about power.

As far as Warren Jeffs is concerned, there is no unhappiness in the FLDS. How can one serve God and be unhappy? Anyone who attempts to usurp the authority of Warren Jeffs will be considered an enemy and be met with resistance. If all are agreed that there are serious problems in the FLDS, then the Attorney General doesn't need Vicky or Anne to do his job, he just needs to exert his power, because power is the only thing Warren Jeffs understands.

The conflict between Vicky and Anne exemplifies the problem in Utah. Vicky points out that Anne is an affluent polygamist, an academic who lives in a nice house, who has always had complete freedom, and all the necessities of life. She has not experienced physical abuse, suffered the oppression of a tyrant, made to share her home with sister-wives and their numerous children, or forced to rely upon welfare to survive.

Polygamy is an emotional subject with the ladies of Tapestry. Over the years they have talked with hundreds of frightened, angry women from all over the United States who have gone through hell. They, themselves, have experienced the worst side of polygamy. Each time they talk with a victim, it's a reminder of their own terrible past. The ladies calling themselves Principle Voices have never been treated like chattel, felt the humiliation of dining with the homeless at the Salvation Army, or lived out of the backseat of an old automobile. Consequently, Tapestry will not compromise their position, they have drawn a line in the sand they will not cross.

I asked Anne if she has been able to establish a line of communication with the FLDS priesthood? She said she had tried with no success. I asked about the Kingston Clan. She said that she met with Paul Kingston and gave him a copy of *Mormon Focus.* At that time Paul said he would *take into consideration* the wisdom of assigning someone from his group to work alongside Anne and her group. I asked about J. LaMoine Jenson, the heir apparent of AUB. She said that AUB was still skittish over their last encounter with the AG's office.

The Attorney General had persuaded Owen Allred into letting his staff speak at one of their meetings. The AG people separated the men from the women and then tried to convince the women to leave polygamy. She said she hadn't made any headway with AUB.

Foremost in the pursuit of solutions has been the phrase, "It's not about religion." That phrase has been repeated so often that it sounds like a slogan. As a catchword, "not about religion" is closer to the truth than government realizes, because in the organized polygamist groups it is *not* about religion, *it is about power.*

The oppression of women in polygamous groups is in direct proportion to the power of the prophet.

Power and oppression go hand in hand. Warren Jeffs of FLDS, followed by Paul Kingston, are the two most patriarchal and exert the most power in any of the groups. The women in both groups *are the most obedient because they have the least power.*

The roles of women in these two groups are well defined and insubordination is not tolerated. Therefore, the leaders of these two groups are not going to let Anne Wilde, an outspoken and aggressive female, represent them or their people.

In the least oppressive groups, AUB and Centennial Park, the prophet shares a portion of his power with elite women who help promote the principle of polygamy. In AUB, Dauna Sandmire, Owen Allred's personal secretary and confidant, has been more influential than most of Owen's apostles. Dauna Sandmire is the unofficial "matriarch" of AUB and is deserving of the title. She is more intelligent and much wiser than most of Owen's apostles.

It is unlikely that LaMoyne Jenson or James Harmston will allow Anne Wilde or any of her group to represent them. Consequently, Anne can only represent a fraction of the polygamist groups subculture. She does not represent the ascetic or austere, she represents the affluent, ladies like herself who are not limited by priesthood domination.

If the polygamists really want equal respect from government and mainstream society, then they are going to have to demonstrate that their theology and their practices ares harmonious with government in protecting civil rights. That's going to be hard for the FLDS to do. Notwithstanding the FLDS right of privacy, it is their *resistance to scrutiny* that attracts scrutiny from the media and causes them to receive the greater amount of publicity.

The United Effort Plan (UEP) is the main source of FLDS power. As Ben Bistline, author and historian suggests, if the people of Colorado City and Hildale were allowed to own the property beneath their homes, they would no longer be under threat of eviction. The people would no longer feel compelled to support the FLDS. Mothers would no longer feel compelled to allow the FLDS priesthood to control the marriages of their daughters. Disgruntled FLDS members would have the freedom of selling their houses and moving away.

The people living at Pinesdale, Montana, and Rocky Ridge, Utah, are living under the same threat as the people at Colorado City. However, neither AUB or the FLDS are about to relinquish control of the property unless it is in their best interest.

Historian Ben Bistline thinks it should be government's job to convince polygamist leaders it is in their best interest, just like government convinced Wilford Woodruff in 1890 that it was in the best interest of the LDS Church to discontinue the practice of polygamy.

Chapter Eleven

Rights of Children vs. Rights of Parents

The controversy over religious tolerance and religious freedom becomes deeper and more complicated each day and may eventually be solved by courts outside of the state of Utah and Arizona.

In York Township, State of Pennsylvania, Stanley Shepp is appealing to the State Supreme Court a decision by a York County Common Pleas Court and Pennsylvania Superior Court that ruled that Shepp was not permitted to teach his daughter about plural marriage.

Karen Muller of the *York Daily Record,* York, Pennsylvania, in an article dated November 19, 2003, did an excellent job in covering a controversy that may have a dramatic impact upon our polygamists, although the Supreme Court decision may be a long time in coming.

Stanley Shepp is a convert to Mormon Fundamentalism and was once the adopted son of Tom Green. I interviewed Stan by telephone in the year 2000, in conjunction with this book. At that time Stan was an estranged "adopted son" and probable witness in Tom Green's prosecution. During our conversation he gave me the impression that he was withdrawing from the fundamentalist subculture because he was very upset with the deception by Tom Green. Tom had apparently lied to Shepp about Linda's age when he married Linda, and in what state Linda had conceived her first child. Now it appears that in far off Pennsylvania Stan Shepp has taken up the Mormon Fundamentalist cause of promoting plural marriage and exercising his constitutional right to teach his ten-year-old daughter Kaylynne that God wants her to become a plural wife.

The mother of Kaylynne, Tracy Roberts, was given custody in 2001. Shepp was given visitation rights and during those visits he taught the child she must be a Fundamentalist.

The 1879 Reynolds decision, acting on the presumption that polygamy was not only illegal but immoral, in essence stated that a person could believe in polygamy but could not practice it. But the ruling did not say anything about teaching polygamy to children.

The Salt Lake Tribune "Dad fights polygamy gag order in court" article by Pamela Manson on Dec. 24, 2003, quotes University of Utah law professor:

> "University of Utah law professor Edwin Firmage, a great-great-grandson of Brigham Young, describes himself as a staunch defender of polygamy and says prosecution of polygamists should be limited to cases of abuse, incest or underage marriage. And, he said, the First Amendment right to free speech extends into the home. But even so, Firmage thinks the girl's mother has reason to worry about her daughter being indoctrinated about polygamy because of the influence a parent has on a child. Although he says it's a close call, the professor agrees with the Pennsylvania judge's gag order based on the circumstances of the case. And, he said, Shepp's daughter can learn about plural marriage when she is older."

In Utah the criminal courts prohibit using "religion" as a defense. The court reasoning was stated by Judge G. Rand Beacham in the sentencing of Rodney Holm, the police officer from Colorado City:

> "Over the course of this litigation, the court has repeatedly ruled that religion is irrelevant to plaintiff's prosecution of defendant. In America, religious belief is neither a criminal act nor a defense to criminal charges. American law distinguishes between religious beliefs and religiously-based

criminal conduct, regardless of whether litigants, the news media or the general public understand that distinction. For this reason, this court has stated that those who want a defendant punished for his religious beliefs or for the beliefs of his neighbors are not just in the wrong courtroom, they are in the wrong country."

But in a civil proceeding there is no such prohibition. In the Kaziah May Hancock civil suit a jury apparently believed that James D. Harmston used the religious Doctrine of Consecration to cheat Hancock out of $250,000. In a transcript of a tape recording in the Hill vs. Allred civil action it was shown that Allred was asked to use his influence as a prophet to ask God what should be done with Virginia Hill's stolen money.

In the case of Stanley Shepp, he has been accused of teaching his ten-year-old daughter that she must be a plural wife in order to please God, and that if she is not obedient to God, she will be damned. That doctrine is clearly Mormon Fundamentalism.

Richard Konkel, the attorney for Tracy Roberts, told the *York Daily Record* that the "question before the court is to what degree a court can direct the spiritual training of a child." The ramifications that will follow will be interesting.

What Shepp is teaching his daughter is being taught by other polygamists to thousands of little girls and boys. These children are being taught that they must grow up and break the laws of the land in order to please God, a must for reaching the highest degree of the celestial kingdom. In essence, what the Pennsylvania Supreme Court will have to decide is if the First Amendment protects a parent's right to teach his child to grow up and break the law.

It may be that the court's decision will be based upon what is best for the child and not what is best for Stan Shepp. In that case, what is being taught is apt be scrutinized with the precision of a magnifying glass, as it should be. As the subject of polygamy becomes more public, it looks like the courts may one day soon be compelled to decide if polygamy is harmful, or more specifically, if the polygamy as taught by Mormon Fundamentalists is harmful when taught to children.

No matter how you look at it, the question is problematic. If Utah and Arizona should decriminalize polygamy between consenting adults, it would imply that there is no harm in teaching it to children. As long as polygamy is a crime under the bigamy statute, it implies that polygamy is harmful and therefore teaching children that they must grow up and live it would be harmful.

How far should our courts go in protecting religious rights? Historian Will Durant, in the third volume of his epic *The Story of Civilization,* said that the ancient Carthagens, a warrior tribe that preceded Christ in what is now Italy, believed they pleased God when they tossed their infant children into a fiery pit. Certain Islamic Fundamentalists are taught that if they blow themselves up along with Israelis or Americans they will be pleasing God. How do we know that teaching little girls to become plural wives is pleasing God? Because Warren Jeffs says so or Stan Shepp, who says God talks to him. There is absolutely no empirical evidence whatsoever to support anyone's claim that God wants women to be plural wives, and if they don't, he will "damn" them.

What effect is that doctrine going to have on the mind of an impressionable child if it is drummed into her head day after day and if her acceptance of that doctrine is a conditional requirement to win the love of the parent? Whether Brian David Mitchell was successful in indoctrinating within a few weeks teenager Elizabeth Smart into submitting as a plural wife is an interesting question. Apparently he made threats against her family. But whatever tool or combination of tools he used, Mitchell was so confident with his programing that he paraded Elizabeth in public within months after she was abducted.

Elizabeth's reluctance or inability to reveal her true identity at the time of her rescue suggests that she had resigned herself to being a plural wife. For nine months, Elizabeth was taught absolute obedience. Part of that obedience involved being a transient and beggar. But then Mitchell was not charged with turning her into an obedient plural wife, he was charged with kidnaping.

In Colorado City young girls the same age as Elizabeth are being indoctrinated the same way. The young girls are taught that God wants them to isolate themselves from the rest of America, give birth to as many babies as their bodies will allow, and use government welfare to feed their children. Pictures taken of Elizabeth while she was under the patriarchal influence of Mitchell showed the look of resignation in her eyes. She was completely in his power. You can see the same look of resignation in the eyes and on the faces of the plural wives in Colorado City. Those are the sour fruits of the FLDS in a country where the pursuit of happiness is held inviolate.

Sufficient education to allow children to draw their own conclusions is often denied. Apostates tell us that children in the FLDS seldom exceed an eighth grade education. In AUB, a college education is discouraged because in the past, educated students have rejected the polygamist way of life. According to Rowenna Erickson, only the elite in the Kingston dynasty are allowed a college education, and only then if they learn skills that will reinforce the power of the dynasty.

In a *Las Vegas Review-Journal* article by Dave Berns, entitled "IN DEPTH: THE DYS-ORDER"

"Despite polygamous family's many financial holdings, some sister wives live like impoverished single mothers. 'My perception is they have the elite run the businesses and give them a chance for an education, but most of the Kingston women, the breeders, live in poverty,' said Ron Barton, an investigator for the Utah attorney general. 'Most of the men aren't supporting their wives or children.'"

The *Ideal* (not the everyday reality) of Mormon Fundamentalism is what Principle Voices is defending. But the validity of their defense is questionable. It is like taking Mark Shurtleff or Terry Goddard to the banks of the Yamuna River in the city of Agra, pointing at the

Taj Mahal, and saying, "This is India," and hoping he is so impressed that he won't notice or remember the wretchedness in the slums.

Anne Wilde doesn't have children who have accepted the polygamist lifestyle. She has never stood in a welfare line or been forced to live with children in a mice-infested trailer in a remote Nevada desert. Nor has Anne had to compete with a sister-wife for the affections of their husband. Vicky Prunty is right when she says Anne Wilde's experience in polygamy has been primarily academic. In fact, Anne has not always been the passive, obedient plural wife that the culture requires. According to Ogden Kraut, Anne rebelled when he took his last plural wife.

Anne Wilde and her cohorts represent the plutocrats and Philosopher Kings of polygamy, not the struggling FLDS plebeians who live hand to mouth a day at a time in a constant state of fear. The fear is induced by the propaganda of their leaders, fear that government is going to take away their children like they did in 1953 and put the fathers in jail.

The best thing that happened in finding solutions to the polygamy problem was when the Utah Legislature dedicated money to the Attorney General to hire a special investigator. The man chosen for the job was Ron Barton, who has proven to be a valuable resource.

It takes more than a familiarity with the law to specialize in an area as sensitive as religion inspired crimes. Barton, who has been dubbed by the media as the "polygamy czar," is non threatening, fair, and considerate of the beliefs of Mormon Fundamentalists. By the same token, if a polygamist man has committed child rape, incest or unlawful sex with a minor, Barton has the skills to build a solid case for the prosecution. He had done so on the Tom Green case.

In spite of Barton's critical role in the execution of solutions, he was excluded from the special meeting held at Centennial Park for the benefit of his boss Mark Shurtleff. Vicky Prunty believes Barton was *purposely excluded* because he would have seen through the illusion. Barton's investigations have brought him face to face with the deplorable side of polygamy. Barton has seen the paltry living conditions and dried the tears of oppressed women as they told him their sordid stories.

Chapter Twelve

Decriminalizing Plural Marriage

Religious freedom is and should be a big issue in America. Our country has many different religions and lifestyles. But when we push a peculiar religion or lifestyle underground, we remove it from public scrutiny.

We have serious issues of abuse among some polygamist families as described in this book and in other books. There is a strong argument that if polygamy were decriminalized, the people choosing a polygamist lifestyle would be more apt to come out into the open, and criminal behavior would diminish.

Some people believe that decriminalization may also be a positive way of compelling men who exploit the welfare system to become accountable and take responsibility for the support of multiple wives and their children. Plural wives forced to masquerade as single mothers should be compelled by government to reveal the identity of the fathers. Those fathers should then be held accountable for the government assistance.

Tom Green was convicted of *Criminal Non Support*. Every polygamist like Tom, who intentionally exploits the welfare system to support his spiritual wives and children, should be prosecuted for criminal non support. Government should not be in the business of subsidizing Mormon fundamentalism or any other religion.

Decriminalization will not *automatically* open up the world for women and children in the more oppressed polygamist societies like Colorado City, *because polygamist leaders will view decriminalization as a threat to their power structure.* However, decriminalization would have a positive effect on the next generation. The more open minded government becomes, the more curiosity the children will have about the outside world. The children in Colorado City are already cognizant of the tyrannical propensities of their leaders. Decriminalization will be like opening welcome doors to mainstream society.

But decriminalization will not work unless measures are taken to compel polygamist men to become accountable for the financial support of their wives and children. Otherwise, a disproportionate segment of the polygamist culture, like Tom Green, will continue to irresponsibly father one child after another with no thought other than welfare as to how he will feed, clothe, and educate the children. Decriminalization cannot be perceived as a free lunch to propagate at government (taxpayer) expense. Decriminalization must be equal to accountability and responsibility.

Nor is decriminalization a panacea for all the abuse and problems created by polygamy, but it may be a good beginning. Decriminalization would send a message that society no longer fears polygamy. The polygamists, in time, would learn they have no reason to fear society.

But it will be an uphill battle with *the leaders* of the organized groups. *They need society to be an enemy.* Having a common enemy draws their people together in fear, gives leaders control because the leaders are going to *protect* their people, *they claim.*

In the long run, decriminalization may be more powerful in discouraging polygamy and combating abuse than a ream full of criminal statutes.

And finally, and perhaps most importantly, if polygamist fathers were legally required to take full responsibility for the financial support of their children, rather than having taxpayers do it for them, changes will come.

Utah Code 76-7-20. Criminal non support.
(1) A person commits criminal non support if, having a spouse, a child, or children under the age of 18 years, he knowingly fails to

provide for the support of the spouse, child, or children when any one of them:

(a) is in needy circumstances; or

(b) would be in needy circumstances but for support received from a source other than the defendant or paid on the defendant's behalf.

(2) Except as provided in Subsection (3), criminal non support is a class A misdemeanor.

(3) Criminal non support is a felony of the third degree if the actor:

(a) has been convicted one or more times of non support, whether in this state, any other state, or any court of the United States;

(b) committed the offense while residing outside of Utah; or

(c) commits the crime of non support in each of 18 individual months within any 24-month period, or the total arrearage is in excess of $10,000.

(4) For purposes of this section "child" includes a child born out of wedlock whose paternity has been admitted by the actor or has been established in a civil suit.

(5) (a) In a prosecution for criminal non support under this section, it is an affirmative defense that the accused is unable to provide support. Voluntary unemployment or underemployment by the defendant does not give rise to that defense.

The above Utah statute has plenty of teeth with which to hold accountable those men who, like Tom Green, are bent upon "bleeding the beast" and living off your tax dollars. And Arizona is now aggressively working toward remedies.

Chapter Thirteen

From Tom Green to Brian David Mitchell

Tom Green

Much has been said in this book about Tom Green. He is a good example of why polygamy was outlawed. Tom is of plebeian extraction with the mind of an intellectual, the manners of an aristocrat, but the morals of an ally cat. He had the brains and knowledge to become a successful man in mainstream society had he been able to keep his testosterone and vanity in check.

The accumulation of young wives dominated his energy as he built his own secret polygamy group with adopted sons. As a charismatic leader he could have attracted adult women, especially if they thought he possessed power. But instead he chose to seduce the daughters of his friends. Tom liked them young which is evident by their tender ages: 12, 13, 14 and 15.

Tom did not openly pursue creating a group of followers until his wives had grown up and matured to where the child-adult contrast was not so obvious. He cut his hair after his wife June left him and drug him into court over a domestic dispute. He was afraid his long hair would give the judge the wrong impression.

The turning point in Tom Green's career as a professional talk show guest, and his portrayal of the intrepid, macho polygamist man, came to an end when *Dateline* converged on Greenhaven determined to ask Tom some poignant questions. The show aired in Utah on April 2, 1999.

Margaret Larson asked Tom if he knowingly was breaking the law. Tom stammered for a few seconds and then said "yes."

Margaret Larson then cornered Juab County Attorney David Leavitt and asked him why Tom Green was allowed to openly and flagrantly practice polygamy in his county.

It was the beginning of Tom's celebrated prosecution that ended in a five-years to life prison sentence. The rest is history.

Nearly every polygamist man who has exhibited his wives on television or in the newspapers has lost his wives. The serene, ideal family he hoped to portray just didn't last.

The first polygamist to lose his wives was Roy Potter, the former Murray City Policeman. The next was Dennis Matthews, a defendant in the Hill vs. Allred lawsuit. Potter lost three wives, Matthews lost four. Both men are presently monogamists.

There are others I won't name. They came and went in the Allred Group and the True & Living Church. The point I want to make is that polygamy may appear to be a bed of rose petals one day, but can suddenly turn into a bed of thorns the following day, and often does.

Tom Green currently resides at the Utah State Prison, Draper, Utah, where he is serving concurrent sentences of 0 to 5 years for bigamy, 0 to 5 years for Criminal Non Support and a 5 to life sentence for Child Rape. Barring appeals, theoretically, he could be paroled after serving five years.

Tom has appealed his bigamy conviction hoping to capitalize on a recent Texas Supreme Court decision that overturned a sodomy conviction of two adult homosexuals making love in the privacy of their bedroom. Tom argued that polygamists should be entitled to the same First Amendment protection. However, the State rebutted Tom's contentions by arguing that Tom's case is inapplicable because his sex partners were under age.

In the meantime, Tom's four wives (the fifth wife, LeeAnn, left Tom) are carrying on the family magazine subscription business, and are concentrating on selling subscriptions to inmates in prisons throughout the country. The wives and their children reside in a large four-plex in a small rural town about twenty miles south of the Utah State Prison. They once welcomed media interviews, but now avoid publicity of any kind.

Brian David Mitchell

Elizabeth Smart was abducted June 5, 2002
and rescued March 12, 2003.

It seems that a few people in Salt Lake City are not satisfied with the known accounts of Elizabeth Smart's abduction and have formed theories of their own. A member of the Kingston Group is convinced that Elizabeth submitted willingly to the coercions of Mitchell. Because Mitchell was attempting to build a polygamist family, a lifestyle my Kingston acquaintance heartily endorses, his sympathies are with Mitchell. Still others suspect that something about the kidnaping is being withheld from the public.

As a detective in the Salt Lake County Sheriff's Office, I specialized in sex crimes investigation. After several years of interviewing rape and molest victims, I was able to detect a false story within minutes. Sex offenders are motivated by needs, drives, fantasies, impulses, and resentments. As a result, their methods are predictable and their behavior stereotyped. Just as an offender's behavior can be stereotyped, so can the reaction and behavior of a victim.

It is the detective who is first on the scene. It is the detective who sees first hand the physical and emotional trauma. It is the detective who patiently helps the victim sort out the confusion and mixed feeling that every sex crime victim experiences. Every female victim of a sexual assault, child and adult, is tormented by thoughts that maybe she should have reacted differently, did she provoke the assault, and what are other people going to think. Lawyers and psychologists interview victims after the fact and form conclusions that either serve their purposes (lawyers) or conform to an established profile (psychologists).

Elizabeth Smart's submissiveness, and the reaction of her little sister, were consistent with the behavior of similar victims. The following is an example of an actual case.

Judy (not her real name), age twelve, was awakened in the middle of the night by a young man with a knife at her throat. He told her to lay still and if she screamed he would kill her. She was petrified. A million things raced through her mind. Would he kill her if she cried for help? Would he harm her parents who were asleep in the next room?

Her assailant, a young man in his mid twenties, was a distant friend of her older brother who was sleeping in the basement. The assailant had been in the house with her brother early the previous morning. As the molester left the bedroom, her father had gotten up to use the bathroom, spotted him in the kitchen, and demanded to know what he was doing. The young man explained that he had forgotten something and needed to get it and didn't want to wake the family. Judy's father, unaware of the molest, let him go.

In the meantime Judy lay in bed still confused, still petrified, and still uncertain what she should do. Finally, an hour after the suspect had left the house, she awakened her father and told him what had happened.

There was no physical trauma like bruises or sperm we could use as evidence. The suspect only fondled with his fingers. In other words, it was her story against his, except we could place him inside the house at a late and unusual hour. There was no question in my mind that she had been molested. The trembling, the tears, the look of terror were all consistent with the crime.

The defendant appeared at the trial groomed and dressed like a Mormon missionary. A skilled defense attorney made the twelve-year-old girl look like a delusional, lying little tramp. I was appalled that the judge and the prosecuting attorney let him get away with it. I noticed female members of the jury glance at the clean cut, good looking young man at the defense table, and I could tell they didn't want to send him to prison. He was found not guilty.

As a law enforcement officer, it was one of the few prosecutions I lost. I was disturbed to say the least, but there was nothing I could do about it. My distress was not so much because I had lost, or that a sex offender went free. I was disgusted with what the defense attorney and jury had done to that little girl.

Sitting helpless and alone on the witness stand, Judy was compelled to relive a terrible experience in the intimidating atmosphere of a courtroom full of strangers. She knew what had happened, she knew how frightened she was, but the jury, people she thought would be on her side, by their verdict told her she was either lying or had imagined the molest. The jury, whether they realized it or not, made Judy a victim a second time.

I have not interviewed Elizabeth Smart or Brian Mitchell. But I have read the newspapers and watched television news. Nevertheless, during twenty-three years as a peace officer I interviewed dozens and dozens of victims and sex offenders. But more importantly, I have over thirty years of experience in the exploration of Mormon Fundamentalism. Putting that together, I believe I have formed an accurate assessment of the Elizabeth Smart kidnaping.

To begin with, Elizabeth was a bonafide kidnap victim. Her behavior and the behavior of her little sister was consistent with other victims.

Why didn't Elizabeth later escape when she obviously had the opportunity, especially when she was approached by a policeman? The claim is made that she wanted to protect her family from what Mitchell had threatened to do to them. And her father stated on the Oprah Winfrey special that to survive, Elizabeth had to go "inside herself." It is amazing in today's enlightened and educated society that anyone should question why she didn't just "run away."

Psychologically and emotionally she was in Mitchell's power. Mitchell had used all the familiar cult brain washing techniques, a combination of intimidation and Mormon fundamentalist doctrine, along with hunger, exhaustion, and loss of dignity to control her and mold her into a submissive plural wife.

Mitchell, who is obviously an intuitively perceptive individual, didn't have to study cult methods to learn brainwashing techniques;

it was already present in the fundamentalist doctrines he studied.

The doctrines used to brainwash victims is standard among all the organized groups. The litany goes as follows: Joseph Smith was a prophet therefore plural marriage must be a true principle. Accept it or be damned. Brigham Young was a prophet and he said plural marriage would never be removed from the earth. Therefore, the LDS Church was wrong when it suspended plural marriage. Because the LDS Church is wrong, the keys of authority were taken away and given to Emanuel. As God's chosen prophet, Emanuel can do no wrong and is endowed with unlimited power.

Elizabeth was an active member of the LDS Church. In a sense, church teachings had already laid a foundation for Mitchell's indoctrination. Mitchell took over where the Church left off. What Elizabeth was forced to endure is the same polygamist inculcation that thousands of other kids trapped in polygamist cults are compelled to endure.

There is one other aspect of this bizarre story that may, and I emphasize may, have contributed to Elizabeth's brainwashing and apparent resignation that she was now a plural wife *and belonged to Mitchell.* The last thing I want to do is cause Elizabeth and her parents further distress, but it's important that law enforcement, future victims, and future converts to Mormon Fundamentalism understand the full dynamics behind the brainwashing and mind control process.

Mitchell has been charged with sexual assault indicating that something happened and it probably happened the night of her abduction.

Contemporary polygamists have been known to seduce vulnerable virgins and after intercourse convince them that they must now marry their seducer or go to hell. This is powerful dogma imposed upon the mind of a religious young lady.

According to refugee women from the FLDS, the marriage is consummated as soon as possible after the ceremony because the act of intercourse has deep psychological effects on the mind of the young virgin. The act of intercourse, even though it may be coerced, has a binding influence between the woman and her seducer. It is a delicate and difficult phenomenon to describe, but within the religious context, she now belongs to him, not out of love, but because her salvation depends upon it. A sacred intimate act has happened between them, a phenomenon that can only be explained in terms of religious belief. This rudimentary explanation may help the reader understand the complexity of Mormonism and Elizabeth's apparent resignation to her plural wife status.

As the Salt Lake City Police found out, the Elizabeth Smart kidnaping was not the typical, statistical abduction. Nevertheless, the motivation behind the abduction and the behavior of the principle parties are explainable.

Twice the name Immanuel, an "itinerant street preacher" had been brought to the attention of the police. According to newspaper and television accounts, the last time was in October 2003. Why didn't the police act more aggressively on the tips? Because the chief suspect Richard Ricci had a criminal record that fit the statistical profile. The possibility that a religious street preacher committed the crime seemed too bizarre to be probable. I might have thought the same.

It is not my intent to second guess, find fault or defend the police investigation, but to help explain why such a bizarre crime with so many twists and turns could happen in a major, metropolitan city.

The Salt Lake City Police were not equipped with sufficient knowledge of the Mormon Fundamentalist subculture. There was no statistical information pointing to a religiously motivated kidnaping. Although Mitchell was a Mormon Fundamentalist by every definition of the term, what he did is an anomaly even in the polygamist subculture. Men have in the past gone outside the subculture to procure wives, but never to my knowledge have they resorted to burglary and kidnaping.

However, there is evidence that he did attempt to procure plural wives by the usual method. He wrote a five page letter, dated

March 1, 2001, to Julie Adkison, a rescued member of the Kingston Clan and attempted to seduce her with his self-styled scripture. The letter bore testimony to his divine calling and attempted to flatter Julie by making her think she was an elect lady called by God to become Mitchell's wife.

Unimpressed by his pious persuasion, Julie wisely rejected Immanuel's advances. If he failed with Julie, it is likely his persuasion failed with other women.

Mitchell's rhetoric was as good as other fundamentalist prophets, men like Harmston, John Shugart, and Ervil LeBaron, but that is all he had to offer. He had no following, no meeting house, and no income. Some photos show him as clean shaven but when he kidnaped Elizabeth he looked more like John the Baptist returning after a decade in the desert. And that may have been part of his plan, to look like an apostle.

Mitchell was well versed in the mysteries of Mormonism. His twenty-seven page epistle entitled *The Seven Diamonds Plus One*, and the letter to Julie is proof of that. Nor are his writings that of an insane man, unless we were to say that Joseph Smith was insane. *The Seven Diamonds Plus One* is offbeat Mormonism, nevertheless, it is Mormonism. Each of the contemporary prophets like Harmston and LeBaron give Mormonism their own special touch.

The white robes and veil were part of Mitchell's special touch. If he had donned a green apron, the symbology to the Mormon Temple would have been obvious. His austerity was more than symbolic piety, he was also on a mission like the 19th Century missionaries, spreading God's word without purse or script.

Mitchell is often referred to as crazy, yes, but crazy like a fox. His performance was not that of an insane man. While Elizabeth was under Mitchell's control he was arrested for breaking and entering in San Diego, and while being videotaped convinced a judge that he had no criminal intent and was a harmless drifter. He was subsequently released. The tape and audio was aired by television stations. You didn't need to have a degree in psychology to see that Mitchell was mentally sound and knew exactly what he was doing.

Mitchell was a law unto himself. It is possible that he may have attempted to enter one or more of the polygamist groups. However, if he claimed to be the "One Mighty & Strong," he would have been less welcome than on the streets of downtown Salt Lake City.

Utah polygamists are well acquainted with the doctrine of the One Mighty and Strong. The following is taken from the Doctrine & Covenants:

> And it shall come to pass that I, the Lord God, will send one mighty and strong, holding the scepter of power in his hand, clothed with light for a covering, whose mouth shall utter words, eternal words; while his bowels shall be a fountain of truth, to set in order the house of God, and to arrange by lot the inheritances of the saints whose names are found, and the names of their fathers, and of their children, enrolled in the book of the law of God... (D&C 85:7)

Men claiming to be the One Mighty and Strong are common in the Mormon Fundamentalist subculture. Ogden Kraut once confided that he knew of forty-two separate men who in his lifetime had claimed to be the One Mighty and Strong. Whether Mitchell made that claim is unknown, but he certainly claimed to have authority consistent with the One Mighty and Strong.

Was Mitchell a man deluded? The word delusion implies an unsound mind but that doesn't necessarily fit either, because there is ample evidence Mitchell knew the difference between right and wrong. Illusion is the better word. Mitchell was a fanatic obsessed with the illusion of grandeur and *immense authority* induced by Fundamentalist doctrine.

Ron and Dan Laffery were enhanced by the same illusion when they cut the throat of their sister-in-law and her infant child. Dan, who did the cutting and is serving a life sentence in the Utah

State Prison, still sticks to his story that he was inspired by God. Ervil LeBaron did not try to hide his illusion that he was the One Mighty and Strong. His sons, daughters, and wives also believed the illusion. He instructed two of his teenaged wives to shoot Rulon Allred.

Finding Elizabeth Smart is a story with a happy ending. She was found. She is back in the arms of her loving family. Many are torn in what they want to happen to Mitchell. They want him to pay, but they also want to spare Elizabeth the necessity of testifying.

Chapter Fourteen

The Potential for Violence

The Illusion of Invulnerability is a phenomenon where by virtue of a person's power, position or status, he believes he is above accountability.

Watergate and President Richard Nixon is an example of the illusion of invulnerability. In many ways Nixon was a good president but because he was the President of the United States, he thought he was above the law.

The prophet or leader of each polygamist group is a monarch or autocrat who believes he is accountable only to God, and that it is he who interprets the will of God. In essence the man is a surrogate God to his people because they believe *he* controls the celestial destiny of the human race and each individual.

In the case of the FLDS, their prophet is characterized by apostates as a despot and a tyrant. Fanatics and zealots tend to gravitate towards polygamist cults. The more isolated they feel from mainstream society, the more violence they mention in their sermons. The more threatened the cult leader feels, the more potential for violence exists. The violence may be aggressive, defensive or self-destructive.

Ervil LeBaron, the Lafferty brothers, Brian David Mitchell, and the bombing of an LDS chapel by the Swapp brothers are examples of aggressive violence. The killing of John Singer by lawmen for resisting arrest and the standoff of the Swapp brothers are examples of defensive violence. The potential for another Waco, Texas, or Ruby Ridge should not be taken lightly.

The Heaven's Gate mass suicide and the Jim Jones, Jonestown mass suicide are examples of self-destructive violence. All the mind-control cult ingredients that led to the mass suicides of Heaven's Gate and Jonestown are already in place in the closed polygamist cults. Those people did not kill themselves because they wanted to end it all, they were told they were moving on to a better life.

On three occasions before Rulon Jeffs died, he called a select 2500 from his 10,000 members and instructed them to buy food and clothes and prepare to be lifted up. A plot of ground had actually been set aside designating the exact place of the gathering and expectant lifting. Before and after the "lifting up" the faithful would need food and clothes. The utmost faithful purchased food in loyal anticipation, but the day before each gathering, Rulon called it off with the excuse that the Lord was giving them more time.

According to Rulon Jeffs, the lifting up out of harm's way was the Lord's method of protecting the elite while he destroyed the rest of humanity. (This expected "saving of righteous people" is similar to what Christians call The Rapture.) Many Mormon Fundamentalists believe the terrible events predicted in the Bible that will precede the Second Coming of Jesus Christ are at the threshold.

Doomsday predictions and rumors of evil conspiracies are so rampant in the fundamentalist subculture that it is almost part of their doctrine. For example, in the 1980s Owen Allred warned that the predicted crash of the American economy was about to occur. Consequently, one of his acolytes quit paying his bills and taxes, and went bankrupt. When the nuclear missile scare was at its peak in the seventies, Allredites were teaching that Salt Lake City had nothing to fear because Owen Allred would stand on main street in downtown Salt Lake, raise his "arms to the square" and using the power of the priesthood, deflect the missiles out of harm's way.

Not all, but many Fundamentalists are anti-Semitics. They think the Holocaust was a fabrication and really didn't happen.

They think that there is a secret cabal called the Illuminati composed of capitalistic Jews who control all the world's resources and provoke wars between nations. They are convinced that presidents, kings, and popes are puppets for the Illuminati. James D. Harmston and other fundamentalists teach that the Nazi promoted book *The Protocols of the Elders of Zion,* a notoriously false chronicle condemning the Jewish race, is a work of fact.

The likelihood of aggressive violence initiated by "leaders" of the prevailing organized groups is remote unless they are backed into a corner. Violence is more apt to come from deluded people like the Laffertys, who without warning suddenly take it upon themselves to avenge the prophet or the principle of plural marriage.

However, there is always the possibility of armed resistance on a grand scale much like occurred at Waco, Texas. The organized fundamentalists sects still believe in the doctrine of Blood Atonement that was preached by early leaders of the LDS Church.

The following are statements made by Brigham Young in a discourse delivered at the "Tabernacle, Great Salt Lake City, February 8, 1857," *Journal of Discourses.* Vol 4, p 219:

> "... he [that] has committed a sin that he knows will deprive him of that exaltation which he desires, and that he cannot attain to it without the shedding of his blood, and also knows that by having his blood shed he will atone for that sin, and be saved and exalted with the Gods, is there a man or woman in this house but what would say, "shed my blood that I may be saved and exalted with the Gods?

> "All mankind love themselves, and let these principles be known by an individual, and he would be glad to have his blood shed. That would be loving themselves, even unto an eternal exaltation. Will you love your brothers or sisters likewise, when they have committed a sin that cannot be atoned for without the shedding of their blood? Will you love that man or woman well enough to shed their blood?

That is what Jesus Christ meant. He never told a man or woman to love their enemies in their wickedness, never."

The late prophet Rulon Jeffs, father of Warren Jeffs, quoted from the above Brigham Young "Blood Atonement" sermon in his book entitled *Purity in the New and Everlasting Covenant of Marriage.*

Fanny Stenhouse in her expose' *Tell It All,* published in 1874, p 312, confirms that Brigham's blood atonement sermon was well known:

The doctrine of the "Blood Atonement" is that the murder of an Apostate is *a deed of love!* If a Saint sees another leave the Church, or if even he only believes that his brother's faith is weakening and that he will apostatize before long, he knows that the soul of his unbelieving brother will be lost if he dies in such a state, and that only by his blood being shed is there any chance of forgiveness for him; it is therefore the kindest action that he can perform toward him to shed his blood — the doing so is a deed of truest love. The nearer, the dearer, the more tenderly loved the sinner is, the greater the affection shown by the shedder of blood — the action is no longer murder or the shedding of innocent blood, for the taint of apostacy takes away its innocence — it is making atonement, not a crime; it is an act of mercy, therefore meritorious.

According to Utah Attorney General Investigator Ron Barton, he uncovered reliable information that FLDS Prophet Warren Jeffs wanted a runaway teenager, Vanessa Rohbock, blood atoned for alleged adultery. Apparently Jeffs sealed Vanessa to a man not of Vanessa's choice and she escaped to Canada before the marriage was consummated. While in Canada she had an affair with a boyfriend, her choice of a husband.

The blood atonement edict was eventually withdrawn when under fear and severe pressure she submitted to Jeffs' tyranny and returned to Colorado City. According to sources, Vanessa was released from the first marriage, but promptly sealed to another man other than her boyfriend. Vanessa's story was covered extensively by the *Phoenix New Times*. According to the *New Times*, when the FLDS attorney Rodney Parker was contacted about "Jeffs' alleged blood atonement order," he refused to comment because the accusation was "insane" and did not "justify a comment."

The FLDS is not the only fundamentalist group that still embraces the blood atonement doctrine. While I was an active member of Apostolic United Brethren, blood atonement was furtively acknowledged as a valid Mormon doctrine. In considering the bloody history of Mormon fundamentalism and the predominance of power over religion, the potential for violence will always be present.

I cannot over emphasize that if one is dealing with polygamist leadership (not the people), he should keep in mind that *the driving force is power*, not religion. The organized group is a religious *society*, much more *society* than religion. *The religion has been transformed into an instrument with which to control the society.* If the power is threatened, polygamist leaders have been known to use whatever means are available to protect that power.

The first line of defense is lying. Lying is a historically valid course of action to protect the prophet and priesthood. Lying to protect the priesthood has been furtively taught in AUB priesthood classes and put to practice in the Virginia Hill vs. Owen A. Allred, et. al., lawsuit. Lying is the first stage leading to blood atonement.

There are anti-polygamy activists who claim to have received death threats. Some anti-polygamy activists are reliable, others are unreliable. There is a tendency for a few activists on both sides of the fence to embellish. The leaders of both AUB and TLC have denied they or their people have made threats. It is always possible that the rumors are the result of an overactive imagination.

I have not personally received any direct threats of violence. However, Rod Williams and I were approached by two separate people within AUB with the story that two men had volunteered to "take us out." One was a big fellow who characterized himself as the Orrin Porter Rockwell of AUB (Rockwell was the bodyguard of Joseph Smith and Brigham Young, who allegedly committed murders when necessary.) The other was a Viet Nam veteran with an unstable personality. I confronted the Viet Nam vet who emphatically denied the rumor.

We also received reliable information that certain people in AUB who have access to the Holy of Holies in the endowment house (temple) have prayed for the destruction of John Llewellyn and Rod Williams. We were also told that a member of the AUB hierarchy, during a sermon at Rocky Ridge, stated that after the Virginia Hill lawsuit was over and done with that steps should be taken to make sure Llewellyn and Williams will never do anything like that again. Owen Allred was tape recorded during a meeting at Motaqua stating that Rod Williams had vowed to destroy him, which was untrue. Remarks like that can be very suggestible to a zealot who believes he has a special mission to protect his prophet.

It has been rumored and passed about among TLC apostates that the TLC has a "hit list." Kaziah May Hancock has a small farm on the outskirts of Manti. She returned home one day to find several .22 caliber bullet holes in the front of her house. The incident was reported to the Sheriff where it apparently died.

Most violence among Mormon Fundamentalists is confined to their own members. Years ago a Pinesdale youth cut his stepfather with a knife during a family fight. Although the wound was superficial, the leaders of Pinesdale were outraged. The boy was the offspring of a second-rate plural wife. He was threatened with castration and thrown into a pit for two days. Two years ago, during an early morning priesthood meeting, a deranged member of AUB cut the throat of the man sitting in front of him. According to Ben Bistline, it is not unusual for second-rate boys to be beaten-up by priesthood police and first-rate boys.

Utah investigators have attempted to serve subpoenas in Hildale, Utah, but have been unable to get past a barricade of armed "zealots that protect the prophet." Mark Shurtleff thinks the zealots are more interested *in frightening would be informants* by demonstrating how they are standing up to "outside law enforcement."

Utah investigators have used caution in their exchange with the zealots, not wanting to touch off another Waco. FLDS dissidents have warned that attempts to arrest Warren Jeffs will result in bloodshed.

According to historian Ben Bistline, Warren Jeffs has invested $400,000 in a security system that includes an eight foot concrete wall around his home and at least four other dwellings, all inside a square city block. That's a pretty plush expenditure for a man whose only known income was school teacher, before he ordered the children to be home taught. It would be interesting to know if Warren Jeffs is still on the school district payroll or if funds from the FLDS or UEP are allocated for his personal consumption.

Taking into consideration the violent past of Mormon Fundamentalists, the willingness of Fundamentalists to protect and follow their prophet at all costs, the question should not be, *is there a possibility of future violence?* The question should be, *when will it occur?*

Let us not forget: In November 1978, 912 men, women and children died of self inflicted poison in a settlement called Jonestown in a remote South American jungle. The victims were members of The People's Temple, a religious cult led by Jim Jones.

In August 1992, the wife of Randy Weaver was killed by a government sniper during a standoff in a remote part of Idaho called Ruby Ridge.

In April 1993, the Branch Davidian religious community compound was attacked by government forces. Eighty-six men, women and children died when the compound was unintentionally set ablaze.

In 1997 thirty-nine members of the religious cult, Heaven's Gate, committed suicide in San Diego. Details of all four of these tragedies are easily found on the Internet.

Conclusion

Everyone loves a happy ending to a story. But there is not a happy ending yet to the abuses in the closed Fundamentalist groups (and some Independents) against thousands of young girls and women, and men too.

The goal for this book was to reach law enforcement officers, government officials, legislators, and you, the everyday citizen, to explain polygamy abuses in such a way that you could gain a clear understanding of what so many girls and women are up against, right here in America. And men too.

It is one thing to read about it or see it on Oprah. But imagine *yourself* or *your child* born into a closed society, told what to believe, and then forced to act on those beliefs, knowing that the priesthood police are outside your door making sure you comply. Knowing that if you don't, you can become homeless. You can lose your job. They can throw you off your land and give your home, the one built with your hard labor and carefully budgeted money, to someone who does comply, *and you are left with nothing.*

Imagine your own young daughter suddenly being taken to a meeting where she is told that the old man towering over her will be her husband, that the marriage will take place the next day, and the union will be consummated right away. Watch the light in her eyes fade as she, like Elizabeth, must go inside herself to live, somewhere safer than the world she is about to enter.

"We were just little girls in odd clothes and funny hair who thought we were going to hell if we didn't obey," recalled Laura Chapman, now 38, who has made a new life in Longmont since fleeing 10 years ago with her five children. "Who would think, right here in the United States of America fathers are trading their daughters away like trophies? It's brainwashing and slavery. It's a complete system of organized crime right in our backyard that for some reason the government has simply chosen to ignore."

If you don't like what is going on, then remove what allows them to continue – the fraudulent welfare money that comes from your pocket, your hard-earned tax dollars. If FLDS is now home schooling their children, we need to take back the taxpayer money allocated for their public school coffers, but is now used for something else. We need to close down the welfare fraud cleverly arranged by the Kingstons. We need to find a realistic and legal way to hold men accountable to support their families, and not make you the taxpayer do it.

No one can force another person to leave an unhealthy lifestyle or belief system. But just as we now have safe houses for women who choose to escape domestic abuse, we can also create a similar system for those who want to leave polygamy. They must have somewhere to go, someone to teach them how to live out in the world.

Let your state congressman know you want something done about this. They focus on issues the public is most concerned about. So let them know you are concerned, that you want procedures put in place to create a realistic way for girls and women to leave if they choose, to give men the right to sell their home and move away. Decriminalize or not, but do something.

Utah, Arizona, and the surrounding states are history rich like no other place in the world because of a couple of interesting guys named Joseph Smith and Brigham Young.

I'm proud of my Mormon past, of my Danish, Welch, Irish, and English ancestors who harkened to the call of Mormonism. They came to this country seeking a better way of life and

Mormonism paved the way. One grandpa was a ship's captain (Tomlison), another pulled a handcart across the plains and down Echo Canyon. One was a polygamist, John Greenleaf Holman, who like me, at one time had three wives, until they started fighting among themselves. Holman was one of the first to settle Pleasant Grove. Rees Rees Llewellyn, the Welchman, was one of the first to settle Fountain Green. And on the Danish side, the Frandsen family settled in the coal rich country of Carbon County. But there is really nothing unusual about my ancestors because most native Utahns or Arizonans can make similar boasts.

Mormons are notorious for bearing their testimonies. Even though I am no longer a Mormon, or a polygamist which I was for twenty years in the AUB, it is only fitting that I conclude this book by testifying that polygamy abuses are wrong.

I do not apologize for my polygamist past. I am one of the lucky ones who emerged on the other side better off than when I entered.

And why am I better off? Because of the children and grandchildren I never would have had. Even though my family split in three different directions when I left polygamy, I still have my kids, and my kids still have me. And when my great grandchildren grow up and read about their great grandfather, I hope they say, "He was an adventurer."

Notes

1 For an excellent, scholastic account of polygamy in the LDS Church after the Manifesto: *Solemn Covenant, The Mormon Polygamous Passage,* B. Carmon Hardy, University of Illinois Press, 1992.

2 There are many literary sources regarding the 1886 visitation, Eight Hour Meeting, and the evolution of the Mormon fundamentalist subculture, but the sources are written either from the LDS Church point of view or the fundamentalist view.

From the Church view I recommend: *The Polygamy Story: Fiction and Fact,* J. Max Anderson, Publishers Press, Salt Lake City, 1979. Anderson's book is out of print but can be found in libraries and rare book sellers.

The Life and Teachings of Lorin C. Woolley, Brian C. Hales, 1993. Brian has done an excellent job of research. The best way to obtain his writings is through his website: www.mormonfundamentalism.com.

For literature from the fundamentalist perspective I recommend Pioneer Press, Ogden Kraut (deceased). Ogden was probably the most articulate and knowledgeable of Utah's fundamentalists. He was a historian, advocate, and author having written dozens of historical accounts pertaining to Mormon fundamentalism. Ogden's publications can be obtained from Anne Wilde.

The 1886 Visitations of Jesus Christ and Joseph Smith To John Taylor, The Centerville Meetings, Lynn L. Bishop, Latter Day Publications, Box 126383, SLC, UT., 84116-0383.

3. The doctrine prohibiting the Black Race from holding the priesthood was not a commandment but inspired policy. *Mormonism and the Negro,* by John J. Stewart, Bookmark, A division of Community Press Publishing Company, Orem, Utah, 1963.

4. In 1977 Ervil had Rulon C. Allred murdered in Murray, Utah. The shooters were two of his young wives. One of the shooters, Rena Chynoweth, after beating the murder prosecution, wrote *The Blood Covenant, The True Story of the Ervil LeBaron Family and its Rampage of Terror and Murder,* Diamond Books, Austin, Texas, 1990.

Ervil harassed the various polygamist groups, attempting to extort tithing for two years prior to Rulon's murder. During that time, while a deputy, I built an extensive intelligence file on Ervil which included photographs of Rena and her sisterwife.

Ervil had Rulon killed to lure his brother, Verlan M. LeBaron, to the funeral where he planned to assassinate him. A car full of Ervil's gunmen drove past the funeral, which was held at Bingham High School, but they aborted the hit because of the security. We had deputies all over the place.

In 1981, Verlan self published his own book *The LeBaron Story.* Ervil was convicted of murder and died in the Utah State Prison of a heart attack in August 1981. Verlan died a short time afterwards in an auto accident.

5. Fundamentalists believe that they have the power to seal plural marriages outside the temple. Not all fundamentalists have erected a temple or endowment house. Those that have try to perform all marriages within the sacrosanctity of the temple. According to fundamentalists, plural marriage is "celestial marriage." But according to the LDS Church, only a temple marriage is celestial marriage.

6. For a comprehensive study of the history of Colorado City: *The Polygamists, A History of Colorado City, Arizona,* Ben Bistline, Agreka Books, 2004.

7. For an excellent account of young girls disappearing see www.helpthechildbrides.com

8. For the information of non Mormons, the "apron" is part of the temple clothes church members wear inside the temple. Jim's apron has a gold hem which he claims sets him apart as the prophet.

9. Calling & Election is a temple ordinance in which the member is assured of a celestial exaltation. Some believe that once a member has received the Calling & Election, he or she can no longer sin. This ordinance is no longer given by the LDS Church.

10. For a complete and fascinating account of the life of the original Virginia Hill: *Bugsy's Baby, The Secret Life of Mob Queen Virginia Hill,* Andy Edmonds, A Birch Lane Press Book, New York, NY, 1993.

11. This information was taken from the court records of Harry Hilf's prosecution.

12. At least two unexpected search warrant raids were executed on Virginia's home in search of evidence.

13. The author has copies of these Trusts in his possession.

14. The Gadianton Robbers were a secret, nefarious organization found in the Book of Mormon.

15. Many Utah polygamists are obsessed with the idea of a "place of refuge" where they can flee from government persecution, or when

the American economy collapses. This is a holdover from the early millennial view of the last days when catastrophes of all sorts will usher in the Second Coming of Jesus Christ.

16. This information was received from AUB member Paul Hess in a tape recorded telephone conversation. Paul said, "Everyone in the suburban except me is a defendant." Later on while on the witness stand, Paul had trouble remembering who was in the suburban.

17. See Juab County Recorder, Entry No. 19108. Red Cedar Corporation is owned by Owen A. Allred, J. LaMoine Jenson, and Glen Allred. It was brought out during the trial that money from AUB tithing goes into the Granite Ranch at the monthly tune of $30,000.00 a month.

18. Until 1995 when fellow investigator Rod Williams, and I discovered Red Cedar Corporation, the AUB membership thought the Granite Ranch was owned by AUB. When the truth was leaked to the membership, only a few members were upset enough to apostatize. Even though the membership had been clearly deceived, the majority stayed loyal because they believed Owen A. Allred held the keys to their exaltation.

19. Shekinah is also spelled Shekineh. The latter spelling seems to have more reference to the feminine spirit, the former spelling "Shekinah" seems to have more to do with a protective spirit or influence.

20. Harmston taught a doctrine called Multiple Mortal Probation, a form of reincarnation.

21. In 1977 the New York legislature enacted a law prohibiting criminals from using their notoriety for profit, commonly called the Son of Sam law. The notorious murderer, David Berkowitz who killed 6 and injured 7, sent letters to the police and newspapers.

Following is an excerpt from one of his letters: *I am deeply hurt by your calling me a woman hater. I am not. But I am a monster. I am the "Son of Sam."* Berkowitz was called the "Son of Sam" killer. The name stuck so it was only appropriate that the law be called the Son of Sam law. Forty-two States and the Federal Government followed New York's lead and enacted similar laws. Utah is not one of them.

22. The figure does not represent the total population of the FLDS. At that time, Rulon Jeffs, the FLDS prophet and leader lived near the mouth of Little Cottonwood Canyon in Salt Lake County. FLDS members were scattered throughout state of Utah and Canada. Before Rulon died, he instructed all faithful members to move to Colorado City or Hildale.

23. *Fifteen Years Among the Mormons,* Nelson Winch Green, H. Dayton, Publisher, New York, 1860

24. *In Sacred Loneliness, The Plural Wives of Joseph Smith,* Todd Compton, Signature Books, Salt Lake City, 1997.

25. *The "Americanization" of Utah for Statehood,* Gustive O. Larson, The Huntington Library, San Marion, California, 1971, p 60 footnote.

26. *Encyclopedia of Mistresses, An Under-the-Covers Look at the "Other Women" of History's Most Influential Men,* Dawn B. Slova, Ph.D, Longmeadow, 1993.

27. *The True Believer,* Eric Hoffer, Harper & Row, 1951. Hoffer describes the phenomenon of mass movements. Hoffer was considered a philosopher. Self educated and called the "stevedore philosopher," he wrote several books and had a regular column in hundreds of newspapers during the sixties. His book is the best source available in understanding the dynamics behind the "true believer."

About the Author

John R. Llewellyn, retired Salt Lake County Sheriff's Lieutenant, specialized in sex crime investigation that included polygamy complaints. He compiled an intelligence file on mass murderer Ervil LeBaron, who in 1977 ordered the death of Dr. Rulon C. Allred, leader of Utah's second largest polygamist group. LeBaron, a self-imposed "One Mighty and Strong," attempted to extort tithing from Utah's polygamist groups.

John's fact-based novel *Murder of a Prophet* is a chronicle of a violent plot by one prophet to unite all polygamists and topple the Mormon Church. Using a paradigm of the Allred murder, it takes the reader through a factual and fascinating expose' of the dark side of Utah polygamist cults. *A Teenager's Tears: When Parents Convert to Polygamy* is a tender, emotionally-charged and moving story that pulls the reader into that world.

In order to best combat and understand the polygamist, deputy Llewellyn studied Mormon doctrine and was converted to Mormonism, and then Mormon Fundamentalism. Impressed with the integrity, virtue and undaunted conviction of many of the polygamists, after his retirement Llewellyn became a member of Apostolic United Brethren. However, when the leadership of Apostolic United Brethren re-postured, claiming "all" the priesthood keys and pretending they were the sole conduit to a celestial exaltation, Llewellyn took a second look at the fundamentalist belief structure and summarily disassociated himself.

Llewellyn, now a muckraker and freelance writer, is recognized as an expert on Mormon Fundamentalism and polygamy. He is also the lead investigator in a lawsuit against polygamist James D. Harmston and his True and Living Church, headquartered at Manti, Utah, as well as a consultant for the Attorney General's Office.

John Llewellyn is uniquely qualified as a polygamy expert and can speak to the issues in a way no one else can. He is highly articulate and thoroughly knowledgeable about law enforcement polygamy strategies, government attitudes, and the vast issues inside and outside of polygamy. He knows all the leaders of polygamy groups, many of their members, and a multitude of polygamists who live outside a group. He is available for interviews by TV and the Press. See his website: www.polygamybooks.com.

John may be contacted via e-mail: jrllewellyn@apcomp.com.

John R. Llewellyn appeared on *The Today Show with Matt Lauer & Katie Couric* August 24, 2001, on *NBC Nightly News with Tom Brokaw*, May 21, 2001, on Fox News Channel's *The Edge* with Paula Zahn June 27, 2002, on MSNBC March 15, 2003, on *Inside Edition* March 17, 2003, and on *Good Morning America* April 4, 2003.

Books About Polygamy

A Teenager's Tears: When Parents Convert to Polygamy
by John R. Llewellyn

Review: Laura Chapman.
"Llewellyn accomplishes the incredible task of exposing the many diverse dynamics of Utah polygamist groups and their members in *A Teenager's Tears*. The characters of the women, children, men and self-proclaimed apostles are both astounding and precise. The display of male privilege, abuse of power in leadership, and struggles within families is triumphantly accurate. The feminists within the groups are still captured in a basic belief that without a man there is no heavenly glory in the hereafter."

Laura Chapman has been featured on CBS *48 Hours*, ABC's *20/20*, and in *The New York Times*, *Los Angeles Times*, and in London newspapers. She grew up in the Colorado City polygamist group as the 25th child of 31 children. After leaving the group, she obtained double degrees in Sociology and Human Development, with a minor in psychology.

Excerpt

Emma didn't know what to say. The last time she saw Mary, she was a sweet, beautiful girl with newfound freedom and plans to become a nurse in a children's hospital. Sweet, gentle, kind Mary.

Emma's heart broke. Before her stood a women old beyond her years. What could she say? But she *had* to know what had happened.

"The last time I saw you, Mary," said Emma carefully, "you were enrolled at Westminister College."

"I know. I'm sorry, Emma. I … I just couldn't do it. I felt like an imposter. It just wasn't me. I finally had to face the truth … I was wrong to try and leave the group. I tried, really I did … but I didn't fit in. Without you and Gwen, I just didn't have what it takes. I'm sorry."

Emma fought back tears. "Oh, Mary, Mary … I should have been there when you needed me."

"I don't blame you," said Mary compassionately. It was the first time she showed any emotion. "And please don't blame yourself. It was something I had to do on my own and just couldn't. I'm back where I belong." There was no regret in her voice, she was merely acknowledging a fact.

Emma wanted to scream, NO, YOU BELONG OUT IN THE WORLD, FREE, MAKING A LIFE.

"Is there still a chance, Mary? I'll help you. I promise … this time I won't let you down."

Mary reached out and touched Emma's arm. "No, thank you. If I didn't have the strength when I was eighteen, I wouldn't have it now."

"Are you sure, Mary?"

Mary heaved a big sigh and pulled the youngest child close to her side. "From the day I was born," she said, "I was taught that I would grow up to be a plural wife. I was told it was the greatest calling a woman could have. I was told only a man holding the priesthood could resurrect me and take me to the celestial kingdom. And I was told that the outside world was Babylon and if I left the group, I would be damned. But … I think the real reason I didn't make it was the uncertainty. Emma, I was scared to death all the time …"

Murder of a Prophet: Dark Side of Utah Polygamy
by John R. Llewellyn

A riveting story of intrigue, murder, and sex. Lusting for worldwide power, the fanatical leader of a Utah polygamist group launches a plan to become the "prophet" over the entire Mormon Church. Detectives fear a doomsday Waco-type standoff with women and children. Investigator John Llewellyn, polygamy expert, creates a fascinating tale of fiction taken from real-life events.

Review: *The Salt Lake Tribune*, Greg Burton, Mar. 23 2000

"John R. Lewellen looks every bit the part he plays in real life: father, retired cop and storyteller, a tweed-coated 66-year-old brimming with the miscellany of crime and impropriety in Utah. He is a character in many of the tales he tells—stories drawn from his days as a sheriff's detective. So it is a bit surprising that his first book is not "real," but a fictionalized drama of doomsday polygamists and that Llewellyn is nowhere to be found on the 180 or so pages.

"Or is he?

"Murder of a Prophet: The Dark Side of Utah Polygamy – published last month by Agreka Books of Sandy – has angered some of the region's polygamists. Leaders in Colorado City, Ariz., and Hilldale, Utah – where the old-time Mormon tenent of "celestial" or plural marriage prevails – have reportedly banned the book.

"Elsewhere, the story, a chronicle of a violent plot to unite all polygamists and topple the Mormon Church, has drawn praise for its true-to-life portrayal of the social fabric of Utah's religious subculture.

" 'I kept looking at the women and the girls he writes about and how real they are,' says Rowena Erickson, a former polygamous wife who fled Utah's Kingston clan and later helped form a support group called Tapestry Against Polygamy. 'He knows the life.' "Llewellyn is everything he purports to be and more. . . ."

The Polygamists: A History of Colorado City, Arizona
by Benjamin Bistline

Agreka Books, 2004. (Expected on the market by March)
Ben Bistline is undoubtedly the most credible and knowledgeable source of information when it comes to polygamy and Colorado

City and all its history. Ben lived it, breathed it, and was there as it all happened.

An energetic man in his early seventies who was raised in Colorado City, he was one of the men who opposed the one-man-rule of Rulon Jeffs and the stranglehold of the United Effort Plan (UEP). Ben has family and friends in both the FLDS and Centennial Park. He is not a polygamist; he is an active member of the LDS Church and serves on the stake high council.

He knows more about the people, their motives, their family connections, their religion, their strengths and their weaknesses than any other pundit. The history of Colorado City and its people, the conditions that drove devout Mormons to a desolate desert, is as dramatic and as important to Utah and Arizona history as the 1890 Manifesto. Ben's book is so well organized and well written that readers assume he is a college professor.

Excerpt

In 1989 I was asked if a history had ever been written about Short Creek (Colorado City, Arizona). I realized that such a history would be important to future generations, because those persons who had seized political and religious control of the community were lying about its history in order to justify their power takeover.

Since I have been associated with the polygamists all my life and have lived in Short Creek since 1945, I supposed I could compile as accurate a history as any other person living here. So I began gathering information and documents. I was able to obtain some important letters written in the forties and fifties due to a lawsuit that was filed in 1987. I also have been able to obtain some journals of the early "Fundamentalist" leaders. This, along with the printed sermons of LeRoy Johnson, polygamist prophet, and several sermons of other leaders, has been the basic source for this history. Very important, however, is the fact that I have been an eyewitness to almost all of this history since the late thirties (I was born in 1935).

One major event greatly influenced me to finish this history.

Martha Sontag-Bradley, a history major at BYU, compiled a somewhat brief history of the 1953 Short Creek raid and a little of the history leading up to it. She spent two or three weeks living in Colorado City, gathering information for her book. This information was all obtained from the "Barlows" and reflected only their view. She failed any attempt to obtain any opposing views, which in my opinion, is a very grave mistake for any author to make.

Since the "Barlows" are those who have "seized" control of the political and religious power in the community, her source of information was very biased and one sided. Her historical "facts" were so grossly in error that the captions under the photographs in the book did not even correctly identify the persons in the pictures.

While reading the book, I became so incensed in regards to the "false facts" recorded, that my determination was renewed to finish this work. That way, there will at least be an opposing historical view of "our" history so future generations will at least have an opportunity to determine for themselves what the truth might be.

My only hope in writing this history is to try and portray that the things told to the followers of the "Fundamentalist Cult" are NOT FACT and that once a person begins to question such, only then will they be able to see the truth in the matter and be able to take steps to break out from under its grasp.

The hold that these religious leaders have on the people and the community is very powerful and even though many of the people suspect that things are not right, it is very hard to make any great change to better their circumstances. Maybe in some small way this history can help those who are seeking to find the truth.

Ben Bistline

All of these books are available through amazon.com, bn.com, other Internet bookselling sites, and may be ordered from your local book store. Ben's book should be available by March 2004.

Printed in the United States
29366LVS00003B/265